# IMAGINING OTHERWISE

Northwestern University
Studies in Phenomenology
and
Existential Philosophy

# IMAGINING OTHERWISE

## Metapsychology and the Analytic A Posteriori

Andrew Cutrofello

Northwestern University Press
Evanston, Illinois

Northwestern University Press
Evanston, Illinois 60208-4210


Printed in the United States of America

ISBN 0-8101-1399-6 cloth
0-8101-1400-3 paper

**Library of Congress Cataloging-in-Publication Data**

Cutrofello, Andrew, 1961–
Imagining otherwise : metapsychology and the analytic a posteriori / Andrew Cutrofello.
p. cm.—(Northwestern University studies in phenomenology and existential philosophy)
Includes bibliographical references and index.
ISBN 0-8101-1399-6 (cloth : alk. paper).—ISBN 0-8101-1400-3 (pbk. : alk. paper)
1. Kant, Immanuel, 1724–1804. Kritik der reinen Vernunft. 2. Psychoanalysis and philosophy. 3. Freud, Sigmund, 1856–1939. 4. Lancan, Jacques, 1901– . I. Title. II. Series: Northwestern University studies in phenomenology & existential philosophy.
B2779.C88 1997
190—dc21 97-6363
CIP

The paper used in this publication meets the minimum requirements of the American National Standard for Information Sciences—Permanence of Paper for Printed Library Materials, ANSI Z39.48–1984.

Zwei Jahrzehente kostest du mir, zehn Jahre verlor ich
Dich zu begreifen und zehn, mich zu befreien von dir.

Two decades you cost me: ten years I lost comprehending you and ten freeing myself from you.

—Friedrich Schiller, *Xenien*

Experience has taught us that psychoanalytic therapy—the freeing of a person from his neurotic symptoms, inhibitions and abnormalities of character—is a lengthy piece of work.

—Sigmund Freud, "Analysis Terminable or Interminable"

# Contents

# Acknowledgments

No doubt my book is best where I do not think to think, and so where the work of others is present in it. But I am quite aware of some influences to which I would like to call explicit attention.

Alison Brown is a an exemplary philosopher. Her book *Fear, Truth, Writing* helped me clarify my thoughts about the relationship between Kantian theory and paranoia. I am lucky to have had Laura Hengehold as a regular interlocutor and reader of my work. Her fascinating work on psychoanalysis and Kant I discuss in these pages. John McCumber's advice and support of this project are greatly appreciated. His critique of Kantian ethics in his book *Poetic Interaction* helped me frame some of my initial thoughts about this project. Dan Price, who read two drafts of this book, made suggestions that were always deeply reflective and challenging. His book, *Without a Woman to Read*, showed me how to think about the crucial Kantian concept of judgment. Cynthia Willett also read a draft of this book, and her recommendations, as ever, were charitable and insightful. Her book, *Maternal Ethics and other Slave Moralities*, has taught me how to think about the limits of both Kantianism and psychoanalysis.

I would also like to acknowledge the following people for their help in different ways at various stages of this project: Loren Adams, Brent Adkins, Jim Blachowicz, Laura Anders Canis, Angela Capodivacca, Mary Caputi, Sinkwan Cheng, Ann Clark, Amilcar Davila, Matt Edgar, John Fritzman, Susan Harris, David Ingram, Heather Kenny, Bruce Merenstein, Tom Parisi, Joshua Rayman (who read a draft and gave me the benefit of his generous criticisms), Dianne Rothleder, Hans Seigfried, Tom Sheehan, J. D. Trout, and David Yandell.

Special thanks go to Megan Cutrofello, who likes to ask "What *is* a being?" and, again, to Dianne Rothleder, whose own philosophical work has helped me become a recovering Kantian. (And a welcome to Quinn Elliott Cutrofello.)

I dedicate this book to my grandmother, Bessie Nurko Carroll (which doesn't mean you have to read it, Grandma!).

# 1

# Introduction: An Inverse Kantianism

> But such replies belong in comedy, and it is high time to replace the Kantian question, "How are synthetic judgments *a priori* possible?" by another question, "Why is belief in such judgments *necessary*?"—and [*nämlich*] to comprehend that such judgments must be *believed* to be true, for the sake [*Zweck*] of the preservation of creatures like ourselves; though they might, of course, be *false* judgments for all that! Or to speak more clearly and coarsely [*grob und gründlich*]: synthetic judgments *a priori* should not "be possible" at all; we have no right to them; in our mouths they are nothing but false judgments. Only, of course, the belief in their truth is necessary, as a foreground belief and visual evidence [*Augenschein*] belonging to the perspective optics of life.
>
> —Nietzsche 1966, 19

The thesis of this book is that there is a very precise, systematic relationship between Immanuel Kant's *Critique of Pure Reason* and the metapsychological theories of Sigmund Freud and Jacques Lacan. By positing the existence of synthetic a priori judgments, Kant opens up the field of transcendental philosophy. This move presupposes, however, that the judgments in question cannot be analytic a posteriori. With this presupposition, Kant forecloses the possibility of metapsychological, rather than transcendental, questions. When metapsychological questioning eventually appears in the works of Freud, Lacan and others, it takes the form, I suggest, of an inverse Kantianism: all of the judgments which Kant takes to be synthetic a priori are questioned as if they were analytic and a posteriori.

My argument, if right, explains why there is a kind of homology between metapsychology and transcendental philosophy, but it also stresses their profound differences. I try to bring this fact out by drawing, in places, on the work of David Hume. Kant treats the limits of experience as transcendental givens; in this way he assures himself of his position in the world as a subject who must obey unfathomable laws of thought. By contrast, Hume treats the limits of experience as fictions, thereby conjuring an experience of the uncanny.

Hume gives expression to this sense of the uncanny—which is not quite Freud's sense—in his account of the anxiety and despair to which his philosophical reflections have given rise:

> I am first affrighted and confounded with that forelorn solitude, in which I am plac'd in my philosophy, and fancy myself some strange uncouth monster, who not being able to mingle and unite in society, has been expell'd all human commerce, and left utterly abandon'd and disconsolate. Fain wou'd I run into the crowd for shelter and warmth; but cannot prevail with myself to mix with such deformity. I call upon others to join me, in order to make a company apart; but no one will hearken to me. Every one keeps at a distance, and dreads that storm, which beats upon me from every side. . . . When I turn my eye inward, I find nothing but doubt and ignorance. All the world conspires to oppose and contradict me; tho' such is my weakness, that I feel all my opinions loosen and fall of themselves, when unsupported by the approbation of others. Every step I take is with hesitation, and every new reflection makes me dread an error and absurdity in my reasoning. (Hume 1978, 264–65)

Everything here bespeaks a profound melancholia brought on by Hume's skeptical conclusions. In fact, he refers to "this philosophical melancholy and delirium" (Hume 1978, 269).

Freud notes that melancholia is a response to loss. Having lost the basis for believing in his everyday assumptions about the world, Hume experiences the sort of alienation from others which Freud associates with a melancholic's withdrawal of libidinal cathexes. As in the experience of melancholia, the extent of loss is deepened by a loss of the sense of self as well as world. This crisis concerning the identity of the subject can be experienced as uncanny (*unheimlich*) because the subject discovers that it is not "at home" with itself, that the nature of its being is not discernible at the level of its consciousness.

Hume's experience of having lost himself suggests the experience of *aphanisis*, a term introduced by Ernest Jones to describe the "fading" of the ego which corresponds to a loss of libido. Giving the term a somewhat different spin, Lacan writes: "Now, *aphanisis* is to be situated in a more radical way at the level at which the subject manifests himself in this movement of disappearance that I have described as lethal. In a quite different way, I have called this movement the *fading* of the subject" (Lacan 1978, 207–8). Lacan's description of *aphanisis* would correspond to Hume's observation that no adequate signifier (impression) of the subject can appear in self-consciousness. Although Hume does not, as does Lacan, invoke here the concept of the unconscious, he does call attention to the radical difference between the subject's everyday idea of itself (roughly: the idea of oneself as ego) and the skeptical philosopher's (or metapsychologist's) insight that, in itself, the subject is not where it takes itself to be.

Lacan associates the experience of *aphanisis* with the way in which subjectivity reveals its structure in hysteria. In this sense, hysteria is to be understood not as an "abnormal" condition but as one possible manifestation of the subject's uncanny relationship to itself. Because psychoanalysis requires that the uncanniness of self-consciousness be made explicit, Lacan describes psychoanalytic practice as carrying out a certain "hysterization of discourse" (Lacan 1985, 161). He represents "the discourse of the hysteric" as follows:

$$\frac{\$}{a} \rightarrow \frac{S_1}{S_2}$$

The "$" represents the "barred" subject—i.e., the subject whose idea of itself would be cut off from what it is in itself. In this diagram, the barred subject is placed in the position of the speaking subject. It is when the subject speaks *as* barred subject—rather than speaking, say, from the standpoint of its symbolic idea of itself as ego ($S_1$)—that its discourse is that of the hysteric. The arrow would indicate the relation between speaker and addressee. In this diagram, therefore, the hysterical subject is represented as addressing the ego. The reason why, for Lacan, psychoanalytic discourse represents the hysterization of speech is that the practicing psychoanalyst attempts to reveal to ego-identified subjects that which can be represented only as a gap in their claim to self-knowledge. By taking up the discourse of the hysteric, the analysand in effect carries out a kind of "metapsychological epoché" that brings it to a sense of the uncanny. It is only insofar as the ego is willing to give up its certainties about itself and the world—as Socrates repeatedly shows—that it becomes capable of a certain type of questioning.

If we were to stipulate that the concept of the unconscious is an abbreviation for the problem of the uncanny, then to say that metapsychology begins from the concept of the unconscious would be to indicate that it has a "problematic" ground rather than a "dogmatic" ground (in Kant's sense of these terms). In this sense, metapsychology is always—necessarily—in crisis. Friedrich Nietzsche's interrogation of the "will to truth" can be read as exemplifying the paradoxical way in which metapsychology can always treat itself as a symptom. But the fact that metapsychology calls for a critique of itself does not make it unthinkable, nor does it make it somehow guilty of the dream of a "total critique." On the contrary, it indicates the untenability of any claim to adopt a critical position outside of the sphere of symptoms (hence Lacan's claim that there is no such thing as a metalanguage). This point can be made another way. Just as the aim of psychoanalysis is not to strengthen the ego but to problematize its status, so the aim of metapsychology is not to strengthen the pretensions of critique but to problematize them.

In clinging to the certainty that either its "I think" or its "I am" is not in any way a symptom of something outside its scope of self-knowledge, the transcendental philosopher is dogmatically inclined to treat the limits of his or her experience as absolute norms supporting and supported by the possibility of synthetic a priori knowledge. The regulative ideal of "adopting a critical position outside the sphere of symptoms" is the pretension of the Kantian transcendental philosopher, and it is this ideal that leads to both its ethical hubris and, paradoxically, its intractable suffering. As Lacan shows, Kant can be read with Sade precisely because of their shared underlying masochism.

Kant approaches the position of the hysterical skeptic insofar as he takes the metaphysical pretensions of reason to be mere illusions—including, notably, the empirical ego's claim to be certain of its existence as a thing in itself. But Kant treats the unity of apperception as transcendental and therefore in no way touched by the contingencies of experience, and this eventually leads toward a rehabilitation of the illusions (or delusions) of reason. To be sure, in the "Refutation of Idealism," he takes the empirical subject—the ego—to result from the empirical consciousness of the permanence of objects in space, but he treats the transcendental subject as an a priori given which makes possible the experience of objects in space in the first place. By making the transcendental subject both "older" than the ego and morally obliged to keep from being contaminated by the empirical—preeminently by the pathology of inclinations—Kant reduces the problematic of *aphanisis* to an affair that has nothing to do with the ego but which solely concerns the transcendental subject's relation to itself as thing in itself. Hence, the experience of the "barred" subject is taken up not from the standpoint of the hysteric, who encounters the uncanny split between the ego and itself, but from the position of the transcendental subject insofar as it imagines itself to be a "something it knows not what."

Lacan's name for the function of a "something I know not what" that serves as the support for the claims of desire or knowledge is "*objet petit a.*" His "discourse of the analyst" suggests a way of representing the subject position of the transcendental philosopher:

$$\frac{a}{S_2} \rightarrow \frac{\$}{S_1}$$

Here, the speaking subject would be the transcendental subject insofar as it imagines itself to be a noumenal "something it knows not what" addressing itself qua barred subject.

Each of Lacan's four discourses is characterized by a "manifest" structure which is represented on the top of these schemata. It is to this that I am limiting my discussion for now. Hume and Kant, I suggest, offer two distinct ways of interrogating the fact that the *cogito* is in the position of a barred subject. Hume takes up the position of the barred subject and addresses the empirical subject (the ego) from this position. Kant takes up the position of the object which the subject takes itself to be as a thing in itself (even though it is cut off from itself) and interrogates the barred subject (the transcendental subject) from this position. By identifying with the hysterical subject, Hume takes up a position which precludes the possibility of ethical dogmatism. Kant, because he identifies with himself as thing in itself—even though he does not know what he is as thing in itself—takes up the position of the subject that is entitled to be dogmatic about ethical matters. Since Kant acknowledges that he does not know what he is as thing in itself, his dogmatism is not the dogmatism of the ego who claims to know what is good; rather it is the dogmatism of the subject who knows only that he is obliged by a good from which he is cut off, a point that both Lacan and Gilles Deleuze bring out (Lacan 1989; Deleuze 1984).

As many commentators have pointed out, there are direct historical connections between transcendental philosophy and metapsychology. Stanley Cavell refers to the direct "paths of inheritance" linking Kant and Freud (Cavell 1987, 393), and Jürgen Habermas similarly reads Freud as continuing the Enlightenment tradition inaugurated by Kant. Whether or not Freud saw himself as directly influenced by Kant, it is clear that he viewed psychoanalysis as contesting many of Kant's claims. An obvious example is Freud's refusal to recognize the categorical imperative as a synthetic judgment springing a priori from human reason (*SE* XIX, 167). Freud sees himself as capable of asking questions that Kant could not—specifically, questions concerning the genesis of structures of experience which, to Kant, appear to be a priori. In tracing the genealogy of such seemingly a priori givens as the categorical imperative, Freud recasts transcendental problems as problems of metapsychology. In this sense, Freud could be said to offer an alternative approach to the Kantian critique of the problems of metaphysics—one that makes the genesis of the illusion of the transcendental (rather than "transcendental illusion" in Kant's sense of this term) its central problem.

Unlike Kant, who dogmatically insists on the correctness of his transcendental framework, Freud sometimes wonders whether he is offering "a myth rather than a scientific explanation" (*SE* XVIII, 57), and he regularly calls attention to the irreducibly speculative character of his hypotheses, as, for example, in the following passage: "What follows is speculation, often far-fetched speculation, which the reader will consider or dismiss according to his individual predilection. It is further an attempt to follow out an idea consistently, out of curiosity to see where it will lead" (*SE* XVIII, 24). In passages such as these, Freud appears to show no interest in "deciding" whether metapsychology should ultimately be treated as science or as myth. One way of resolving the matter, of course, would be to construe metapsychology as a strictly Kantian enterprise. This seems to be Paul Ricouer's reading of Freud. Arguing that "the concepts of analysis are to be judged according to their status as conditions of the possibility of analytic experience," Ricoeur writes:

> One may, if he so wishes, speak of "deduction," but in a "transcendental" and not in a "formal" sense; deduction is concerned here with what Kant calls the *quaestio juris*; the concepts of analytic theory are the notions that must be elaborated so that one may order and systematize analytic experience; I will call them *the conditions of possibility of a semantics of desire.* (Ricoeur 1970, 375)

An obvious advantage of Ricoeur's reading is that it clarifies the nonpositivistic character of metapsychology. A disadvantage is that it dogmatically presumes that there is an a priori transcendental logic governing a semantics of desire. Not surprisingly, Ricoeur explicitly associates Freudian theory with the work of Kant rather than Hume; concerning Freud's theory of drives, he writes: "This dynamic point of view has long prevailed over the preconceptions of the old empirical psychology and its *tabula rasa*; psychology has opted for Kant and against Hume" (Ricoeur 1970, 351). One obvious problem with this reading, however (a point to which I will return), is that Hume simply does not have a *tabula rasa* view of the mind; the principles of association of ideas are not acquired through experience.

Both Freud and Hume make use of tentative, speculative assumptions in their attempts to account for the genesis of the ideas of space and time. But these assumptions have no dogmatic or transcendental status. For example, Hume at one point suggests that the cause of the mind's tendency to confusion might be explained in terms of how the "animal spirits" in the brain work:

> I shall therefore observe, that as the mind is endow'd with a power of exciting any idea it pleases; whenever it dispatches spirits into that region of the brain, in which the idea is plac'd; these spirits always excite the idea, when they run precisely into the proper traces, and rummage that cell, which belongs to the idea. But as their motion is seldom direct, and naturally turns a little to the one side or the other; for this reason the animal spirits, falling into the contiguous traces, present other related ideas in lieu of that which the mind desir'd to survey. This change we are not always sensible of; but continuing still the same train of thought, make use of the related idea, which is presented to us, and employ it in our reasoning, as if it were the same with what we demanded. This is the cause of many mistakes and sophisms in philosophy; as will naturally be imagin'd, and as it wou'd be easy to shew, if there was occasion. (Hume 1978, 60–61)

It would be worth comparing what Hume has to say here on the subject of the paths along which the animal spirits move with Freud's account of the system of facilitations (*Bahnungen*) in his "Project" essay of 1895 (*SE* I). It would also be interesting to compare Hume's speculations with Freud's speculations on the primitive organism and its acquisition of ideas of time and space. There are definite parallels not only with respect to content but with respect to the ways in which Freud and Hume avail themselves of scientific hypotheses without thereby committing themselves to any form of dogmatic realism (either empirical or transcendental).

If it is not surprising to find structural affinities between metapsychology and Kantian philosophy, then, the question is whether these affinities bespeak a fundamental agreement between the two (as some have claimed) or whether they arise from metapsychology's attempt to speculate on the causes of Kantian symptoms. Although I will be arguing for the latter interpretation, the issue is complicated, and would ultimately bear both on issues concerning transference and countertransference in psychoanalysis and on the issue of whether there can be such a thing as a metalanguage proper to metapsychology.

My suspicion is that there is at work in the history of metapsychology something on the order of a repetition compulsion which has perhaps kept psychoanalytic theorists from adequately questioning this Kantian inheritance. This is a topic to which I will return in the last chapter of this book. Here I will simply lay out the contours of this question as it bears on Lacanian theory in particular.

Although he takes psychoanalysis to bring about a (Humean) hysterization of the discourse of the analysand, Lacan also identifies the position of the metapsychologist with that of the (Kantian) discourse of the analyst. Perhaps as a result, some commentators, such as Slavoj Žižek and Joan Copjec, have emphasized some of the Kantian aspects of Lacanian theory. Žižek explicitly argues that the work of Lacan is best read as a kind of transcendental philosophy of its own (Žižek 1993, 3).

But Lacan does not himself cast metapsychological work as transcendental; in fact, in his essay "Kant with Sade," he suggests that only an "impure" critique of reason would be possible after Freud (Lacan 1989, 63). More in the tradition of Hume than of Kant, I claim, Lacan could be said to take the central questions of critique to be genetic rather than transcendental ones. What Freud and Lacan ultimately give us is an account of the formation of impure fictions, not of the timelessness of pure truths. Precisely for this reason, metapsychology can be said to have laid the groundwork for a sort of Humean "antithetic" to the claims of Kant's first *Critique.* I use this term in Kant's sense of a conflict within reason itself. For Kant, there can be no genuine antithetic of reason other than the merely apparent antithetic of the antinomies. An antinomy represents a conflict that reason can resolve; a genuine antithetic would be insoluble. The source of each of the antinomies is a conflict between dogmatism and skepticism; in each case, Kant takes skepticism to represent the Humean challenge to the claims of pure reason. Insofar as he claims to have solved the antinomies, Kant takes himself to have dispelled the Humean threat. Reason must give up the dogmatism of its theses, but it can preserve the possible legitimacy of its most cherished ideas and thereby avoid its own "euthanasia" (A407/B434). I will argue that metapsychology suggests a way of sharpening the Humean challenge to Kant, and so of developing an antithetic to the entire Kantian project.

Such an antithetic would interrogate the Kantian-Lacanian discourse of the analyst from the skeptical standpoint of the discourse of the hysteric. This is not to claim that the discourse of the hysteric represents an ultimate court of appeal. Assuming that every possible discursive position can be treated as symptomatic, we can expect to find it necessary to shift from one critical position to another, with each reflecting discourse becoming the object of reflection of another discourse. Lacan's model of a spinning "wheel of discourses," moreover, suggests that his own position is more subtle than that of a simple identification with the discursive mode of Kantian critique.

On my reading, then, metapsychology develops as a systematic challenge to Kant's thesis concerning the synthetic a priori. Therefore, as I will now try to show, the guiding question of metapsychology will be not "How are synthetic a priori judgments possible?" but "How are analytic a posteriori judgments possible?"

Kant's critical philosophy purports to begin with the discovery that not all judgments are either analytic and a priori or synthetic and a posteriori. There is, according to Kant, a third class of judgments which cuts across this division. The unique judgments in question are intimately bound up with the limits of experience and render problematic the assumption that such experience has direct access to things in themselves. What exactly is the nature of these peculiar judgments? Kant assumes that the only way to interpret them is as synthetic a priori.

At the heart of transcendental philosophy, then, is the wedge Kant introduces to separate the a priori/a posteriori distinction from the analytic/synthetic distinction. The first of these distinctions he defines as follows: "we shall understand by *a priori* knowledge, not knowledge independent of this or that experience, but knowledge absolutely independent of all experience. Opposed to it is empirical knowledge, which is knowledge possible only *a posteriori*, that is, through experience" (B2–3). Kant takes this distinction to be uncontroversial. On the other hand, he claims to be the first philosopher to have recognized the difference between analytic and synthetic judgments:

> In all judgments in which the relation of a subject to the predicate is thought . . . this relation is possible in two different ways. Either the predicate B belongs to the subject A, as something which is (covertly) contained in this concept A; or B lies outside the concept A, although it does indeed stand in connection with it. In the one case I entitle the judgment analytic, in the other synthetic. (A6–7/B10)

Analytic judgments are "explicative" in that their predicates merely bring out what is already contained in their subjects; synthetic judgments are "ampliative" in that their predicates attach some new concept to their subjects (A7/B11).

Many commentators have wondered whether Kant could legitimately claim to be the first philosopher to introduce the analytic/synthetic distinction. Both Hume's distinction between judgments concerning relations of ideas and judgments concerning matters of fact and G. W. Leibniz's comparable distinction between truths of reason and truths of fact are often invoked in this context. But in these cases, Kant suggests, the distinctions in question ultimately collapse into the a priori/a posteriori distinction—i.e., the contrast between judgments whose truth or falsity can be shown independently of experience and judgments whose truth or falsity can be determined on the basis of experience alone. The analytic/synthetic distinction concerns merely the form of a judgment, not its relation to experience. By not recognizing that there was an entirely independent distinction to be drawn here, Kant thinks, his predecessors could offer only variations on the a priori/a posteriori distinction itself.

Kant goes on to state that all analytic judgments must be a priori, and are therefore in no need of empirical confirmation: "Since, in framing the judgment, I must not go outside my concept, there is no need to appeal to the testimony of experience in support" (B11). It is, on the other hand, possible to "exhibit" an analytic judgment in intuition (B17). An example of this would be to draw a triangle and note that it is equal to itself. But exhibiting the truth of an analytic judgment and claiming to verify its truth thereby are two different things. Although I can exhibit the truth that all bachelors are unmarried by presenting an unmarried bachelor, Kant suggests, no one would ever take a survey of bachelors with an eye toward finding out how many of them are unmarried. Strictly speaking it is not impossible to take such a survey; but the moment that one thinks this is how to find out whether bachelors are married or not, one must have made a mistake of some sort. Perhaps one has forgotten or failed to notice that the judgment "All bachelors are unmarried" is analytically true. This would be like cases of weakness of will, where someone pursues something he or she "knows" to be bad only on the assumption of a temporary lapse of knowledge. The point to be noticed, however, is that while it would be *strange* to look to experience to confirm an analytic judgment it is not strictly speaking *impossible* to do so. Thus Kant says only that "it would be absurd [*ungereimt*] to found an analytic judgment on experience" (B11). While it is conceivable that someone might look to experience to seek to confirm the truth of an analytic judgment, such an effort would be evidence of a cognitive fault of some kind. Kant's *Anthropology from a Pragmatic Point of View* suggests two specific possibilities here: "Faults of the cognitive power are either *mental deficiencies* or *mental illnesses*" (Kant 1974, 73). This is a point to which I will return.

Having dismissed the possibility of there being any "normal" analytic a posteriori judgments, Kant asks whether any synthetic judgments are possible a priori, or whether all must be a posteriori. On this question, Kant proceeds in a different manner. He does not say that to affirm the truth of a synthetic judgment without looking to experience would be "absurd"; he says that such judgments would pose a riddle for philosophical thought—namely, the question of *how* they could be possible. Thus, Kant's treatment of the two questions is asymmetrical (one might even be tempted to call it, in the literal sense of the term, "*ungereimt*": *unrhymed*).

He has taken the strangeness of analytic a posteriori judgments to count as a priori evidence against their possibility, and taken the strangeness of synthetic a priori judgments as a reason for puzzling over their possibility.

The road to critique forks right here, though Kant takes no notice of it. Why he should fail to notice this is itself a bit puzzling. After all, if Kant truly is, as he thinks, the first philosopher to discover the analytic/synthetic distinction, it can only be because the idea that there are synthetic a priori judgments must appear, prima facie, to be as absurd as the idea that there could be analytic a posteriori judgments. Those of his readers encountering the analytic/synthetic distinction for the first time—i.e., all of his contemporary readers—would have (again, prima facie) no more reason to dismiss the analytic a posteriori as absurd than they would the synthetic a priori. Why, then, does Kant assume his readers will agree that the way to transcendental philosophy is opened up along one path but that the other path can only be a dead end?

Were we to pursue the trail of this supposed dead end and ask under what conditions a "normal" analytic a posteriori judgment might be possible, a number of possible results of this deviation might be anticipated. First, we might find rather quickly that Kant was simply right to dismiss the possibility of analytic a posteriori judgments. Alternatively, we might find that such judgments are "problematic" in Kant's technical sense of this term, or even possible, but that we can cite no definite examples of any. A third possibility is that we might discover an entire body of analytic a posteriori judgments to be placed alongside the body of synthetic a priori judgments which Kant professes to discover; we might then work out a system that would fit in with the Kantian architectonic—even if only as an adjoining outhouse. Perhaps, more ambitiously, we might find the grounds for writing something like a fourth Critique, one that would suggest solutions to problems posed in the first *Critique*.

For example, in an interesting attempt to link together the works of Kant and Saul Kripke, Stephen Palmquist suggests that "Kripke's analysis of the contingent a priori awakens the Kantian to the possibility of *analytic a posteriori knowledge*" (Palmquist, 270). Palmquist tries to show how Kantian epistemology can accommodate the analytic a posteriori as a fourth kind of knowledge. Contrasting his sense of the analytic a posteriori with the synthetic a priori, Palmquist writes:

> The synthetic a priori and analytic a posteriori are . . . similar classes of knowledge insofar as both are concerned with conditions imposed on the world by the subject . . . but they differ by virtue of the fact that one imposes *general* conditions (a priori) with intuitive (synthetic) content,

> whereas the other imposes *particular* conditions (a posteriori) with conceptual (analytic) content. (Palmquist 1987, 273)

As an example of an analytic a posteriori judgment, Palmquist sketches a situation in which a child learns to say "stove hot" without realizing that the term "hot" could be applied to other things as well. This child could be said to possess analytic a posteriori knowledge. Once she learns that there are other things that are hot besides the stove, the knowledge could become synthetic a posteriori (Palmquist 1987, 274). Palmquist's account squares nicely with a sense of the analytic a posteriori that Kant might accept—i.e., with a sense that would be compatible with the distinct category of the synthetic a priori.

But there is another possibility to consider as well. What if it should turn out that, as soon as we started considering possible candidates for the title of "analytic a posteriori judgments," we found ourselves disputing with Kant over the very judgments which he considers to be synthetic a priori?

Kant himself seems to anticipate and brush aside this problem. For although he denies that there can be any analytic a posteriori judgments, he suggests that it might be possible to adopt a kind of analytic a posteriori approach to the synthetic a priori. He makes this point in the second edition of the *Critique*, where he is concerned to show how the scholastic principle, *quodlibet ens est unum, verum, bonum*, can be understood from the standpoint of his critical philosophy. Kant suggests that the principle be viewed as a special application of the categories of quantity to all knowledge, for in all knowledge there can be found

> *unity* of concept, which may be entitled *qualitative unity* . . . *truth*, in respect of its consequences [which] might be entitled the *qualitative plurality* of characters, which belong to a concept as to a common ground (but are not thought in it, as quantity. Thirdly, and lastly, there is *perfection* [which] . . . may be entitled the *qualitative completeness* (totality). (B114)

Kant's argument is best understood if we keep in mind his understanding of logic in general as a doctrine of concepts, but the analysis of concepts presented here can also be applied to hypotheses. A particular judgment, the hypothesis, will have qualitative unity inasmuch as it subsumes under it a manifold of possible cases. It will have qualitative plurality insofar as many truths can be deduced from it. Finally, its qualitative completeness will consist in the totality of these truths, understood as following from the hypothesis.

Kant goes on to note that one can start with a grasp of the qualitative completeness of a hypothesis and work backwards to the hypothesis itself, "and so in an *a posteriori* analytic manner give us back and accord with what has previously been thought in a synthetic *a priori* manner" (B115). What Kant seems to have in mind is this. Take the judgment that "in all changes of the material world the quantity of matter remains unchanged" (B17). On Kant's reading, this is a synthetic a priori judgment whose possibility must be accounted for. From this judgment, we can deduce a number of conclusions and we can grasp the totality of these conclusions as following from that single principle which is stated in the hypothesis. Once having grasped this latter point, we can "forget" that we have deduced it from the hypothesis and then work backwards from the conclusion to the hypothesis. In this way, it would seem *as if* we had arrived at the hypothesis by way of an analytic a posteriori argument; for we would have started from facts which, taken by themselves, would be contingent truths of experience, and deduced from them a necessary truth.

What is fascinating about this short passage is that in it Kant seems to countenance the possibility that there might be "normal" analytic a posteriori judgments after all. But the main thrust of his remarks suggests that such a judgment would be possible only as a kind of degenerate version of a synthetic a priori judgment. Minimally, the synthetic a priori form would take precedence, which is why *its* possibility is what has to be explained. Thus, Kant thinks he can avoid the slippery slope of "chicken and egg" problems here. But suppose we were to say to Kant, How can you be sure that it isn't the other way around? Why couldn't the synthetic a priori hypothesis be viewed as a degenerate version of an analytic a posteriori judgment? Why couldn't it turn out to be the analytic a posteriori whose possibility has to be explained?

Kant's answer to these questions can be found, once again, in the second edition—specifically, in the B Deduction argument that all acts of analysis presuppose acts of synthesis:

> But the combination (*conjunctio*) of a manifold in general can never come to us through the senses. . . . For it is an act of spontaneity of the faculty of representation [*Vorstellungskraft*]. . . . To this act the general title "synthesis" may be assigned, as indicating that we cannot represent to ourselves anything as combined in the object which we have not ourselves previously combined. . . . For where the understanding has not previously combined, it cannot dissolve, since only as having been combined *by the understanding* can anything that allows of analysis be given to the faculty of representation. (B129–30)

The argument here is tricky and bears on an apparent conflict between a point Kant makes in the Transcendental Aesthetic and a point he makes in the section on the Axioms of Intuition, as well as on how this conflict gets resolved in the Second Antinomy. In the Aesthetic, Kant maintains that "space is represented as an infinite *given* magnitude" (B39). Every space, no matter how small, is made up of parts; to this extent, we do not first encounter a multiplicity of infinitesimally small spaces which we then synthesize into an intuition of a space. Given this claim, it is not clear why a prior act of synthesis should precede our analysis of spaces into their component parts. However, when he discusses the principles of the understanding, Kant argues that we can think of an extensive magnitude only by conceiving it as a synthesis of parts. "I entitle a magnitude extensive when the representation of the parts makes possible, and therefore necessarily precedes, the representation of the whole" (A162/B203). In principle, there is no conflict between these two claims, since the former specifies a criterion of intuition for the faculty of sensibility and the latter specifies a criterion of thought for the faculty of understanding. Kant will call attention to this dichotomy when proposing a solution to the antinomy which concerns the infinite divisibility of space. The idea of "the simple" is a regulative concept for the understanding, but it is one for which no possible object can be given in experience.

It is worth stressing that the solution to the Second Antinomy rests, in effect, on an irreducible difference between sensibility and the understanding. According to Kant, intuitions present us with totalities which the understanding requires us to think of as syntheses made out of irreducibly simple parts. But the fact that the idea of the simple has a merely regulative and not a constitutive function underscores the fact that neither the objects we intuit nor our intuitions themselves could ever have been a presynthesized aggregate. What this would seem to suggest is that it is only a fiction of the understanding to make its acts of synthesis prior to its acts of analysis. That is, all Kant can show is that the understanding *must think* of itself as having first combined whatever it analyzes. The force of this "must" would be based on a regulative ideal, and yet the ideal itself would in turn be justified only if we presuppose that the "must" is constitutive rather than regulative. From the fact that intuitions are always already totalities, we could conclude not that they have first been worked over by the understanding, but, on the contrary, that the understanding itself never synthesizes without first having analyzed. Thus, the alleged priority of synthesis over analysis could at most have subjective validity only, not objective validity. More important, even this subjective validity would have no claim to universality if it turned out that, without the constitutive priority of the principle of synthesis, we cannot prove that the "strange" judgments we make are best characterized as synthetic a priori.

Had Kant pursued this line of reasoning, he might better have appreciated what Hume had been up to. In the *Prolegomena,* Kant suggests that Hume must have recognized the existence, but not the legitimacy, of synthetic a priori judgments: "what [Hume] said was equivalent to this: that pure mathematics contains only analytic, but metaphysics synthetic, *a priori* judgments" (Kant 1977, 15). On Kant's reading, it is only because Hume did not recognize that mathematics yields synthetic a priori knowledge that he was unable to recognize the validity of synthetic a priori judgments elsewhere: "For how is it possible, says that acute man, that when a concept is given me I can go beyond it and connect [*verknüpfen*] with it another which is not contained in it, in such a manner as if the latter *necessarily* belonged to the former?" (Kant 1977, 22). In crediting Hume with recognizing the synthetic a priori character of judgments concerning causality, Kant seems prepared to acknowledge that Hume must have appreciated the significance of the analytic/synthetic distinction. Because he did not recognize that mathematical knowledge was synthetic a priori and because as a consequence he did not suspect that the concept of causality was pure rather than empirical, Hume had no choice but to treat the synthetic a priori in general as being just as "absurd" as Kant treats the analytic a posteriori.

But would Hume in fact agree with Kant that judgments about causality are synthetic and a priori? It seems more plausible to read him as noting that we treat the judgment that every event has a cause as analytic—a fact which is strange not because no possible evidence could count against it but because the judgment is so clearly a posteriori as well. Only experience, Hume argues, could possibly give rise to the idea that two distinct impressions are necessarily connected. This is not to conflate the question of whether a concept is pure or empirical with the question of whether a judgment is a priori or a posteriori. Hume's point is simply that the idea of causality is the idea of a necessary relation between objects the ideas of which are distinct, and so which the mind cannot connect in an a priori way. Given the "obvious" a posteriori character of judgments about causality, Hume's puzzle is why we should treat these judgments as if they carried with them a sense of necessity (Hume 1978, 78). His subsequent argument could therefore be characterized as a critique of the analytic a posteriori, not an anticipation of Kant's critique of the synthetic a priori.

Perhaps the question of whether to characterize a particular judgment as synthetic a priori or as analytic a posteriori could be decided only if we could independently ascertain whether the principle of analysis or the principle of synthesis should be granted priority. Kant thinks the answer is clear. But what if it turned out that he can treat the principle of synthesis as higher only on the basis of having already decided to treat the "strange" judgments in question as synthetic a priori in the first place? Or, to turn the question around, what if in order to identify a particular judgment as synthetic a priori we had to presuppose that the conditions for its possibility were already given? This, of course, is Nietzsche's objection to transcendental philosophy: Kant surreptitiously presupposes the very things he professes to prove. Suppose we had to presume the transcendental ideality of space and time in order to recognize mathematical judgments as synthetic a priori. Were we simply to reject the transcendental ideality thesis, could we not treat mathematical judgments differently? The history of post-Kantian philosophy of mathematics is based precisely on this sort of reasoning; the attempt to reduce mathematics to logic, and thereby to view mathematical judgments as analytic a priori was motivated, in part, by a rejection of Kant's conclusions. The same can be said for Mill's attempt to show that mathematical knowledge is synthetic a posteriori.

In the next chapter I will argue that for Hume mathematics does in fact consist of analytic a posteriori judgments. For now I simply want to call attention to the plausibility of this kind of hypothesis. Suppose we take the judgment "7 + 5 = 12," and assume for argument's sake that the principle of analysis should be accorded higher status than the principle of synthesis. Suppose, further, that we were to treat this judgment as one whose truth can be decided on the basis of concepts alone. The judgment, then, would be analytic. But imagine, now, a person who has learned the basic rules of arithmetic by concepts alone, someone who has never applied these concepts to intuition—e.g., by counting her fingers or toy blocks or coins or anything else. Would we not expect this person to be curious as to whether actual experience would bear out what theory tells her to be indubitably true? Suppose she has been forbidden, by an evil Fregean, from ever appealing to empirical intuitions. Can we not imagine that, when her mentor has turned his back for a moment, she is tempted to carry out a little experiment? And could we not say that a condition for the possibility of her curiosity lies with the gap—however small—between her certainty of the truth of the judgment and her certainty that experience will bear it out? In imagining this, are we not simply taking seriously Kant's own insistence on the radical separation between concepts and intuitions? If this thought-experiment is convincing, it presents a plausible picture of why we might characterize "7 + 5 = 12" as an analytic a posteriori judgment rather than as a synthetic a priori judgment. But can we say which perspective is right?

Rather than attempt to settle disputes of this sort, it might be possible to displace them—as, for example, W. V. Quine does in his famous essay, "Two Dogmas of Empiricism." Quine's strategy is to show that the difference between an analytic judgment and a synthetic judgment is only one of degree, having to do with the willingness of a subject to give up a particular belief (Quine 1980, 43). Only if no possible experience could lead me to retract a certain judgment I have made would this judgment function in my system of beliefs as analytic. If, on the other hand, I were willing to give up the judgment in the face of any evidence against it whatsoever, then my judgment would be synthetic. Construed in this way, however, no judgments will turn out to be either purely analytic or purely synthetic. The most one can do is distinguish between a subject's degrees of conviction concerning particular beliefs. As Michael Dummett points out, this does not mean that the analytic/synthetic distinction collapses; it simply means that as a matter of fact "there are no analytic sentences, and there are no synthetic ones" (Dummett 1978, 375).

Quine's approach enables us to discard the question of whether a particular judgment just "is" analytic or synthetic without foreclosing the question of whether a particular judgment is analytic or synthetic *for a particular subject's web of beliefs.* Here I want to focus on Quine's account of what it would be for a statement to be analytic—it would have to be a judgment that a subject would not be prepared to give up under any circumstances whatsoever. It is worth stressing Dummett's point: Quine has not shown that it is impossible for a judgment to be analytic for a subject in this sense; he has simply shown that it would be strange if someone actually did hold a judgment against which no possible evidence could count. As in the case of Kant's argument against the analytic a posteriori, Quine's argument against there being any analytic judgments rests on his assumption that no "normal" web of beliefs would contain such a statement. (For Quine's regular, but unthematized, appeal to standards of normality, cf. Cutrofello 1992)

But what if there were "abnormal" webs of beliefs—such as the web of beliefs of someone whom Kant would classify as suffering from a "mental deficiency" or "mental illness"? Kant divides the category of mental illness into cases of "morbid anxiety" and "mental derangement" (Kant 1974, 82). Mental derangement he subdivides into three basic types: "its *turbulent,* its *methodic,* and its *systematic* forms" (Kant 1974, 84). In turbulent derangement, which Kant calls *Unsinnigkeit,* the subject is said to be incapable of arranging his or her judgments in any coherent form. By contrast, in both methodic derangement (dementia, or *Wahnsinn*) and systematic derangement (*Aberwitz*) subjects are said to adopt principles which fly in the face of empirical experience (Kant 1974, 85).

Of particular interest is systematic derangement, in which the subject might even judge the impossible to be possible: "It is within his power to discover how to square the circle, to invent perpetual motion, to unveil the supersensible forces of nature and to understand the mystery of the trinity" (Kant 1974, 85).

A deranged subject could well hold to a particular set of beliefs even in the face of what a "normal" person would call sufficient disconfirming evidence. How are we to explain such behavior? It is precisely here, of course, that the specificity of psychoanalytic questioning arises—and Kant clearly sees himself as a "normal" subject capable of psychoanalyzing "abnormal" subjects. But Kant sidesteps the prior question of how I, the critical subject, can tell whether I am a normal or an abnormal subject. At issue is the question that Descartes poses in his first Meditation: How do I know that I myself am not mad? In principle, transcendental philosophy should not be exempt from this challenge, but Kant has very little to say on the topic. It is for this reason, in part, that contemporary admirers of his work such as K. L. Reinhold and J. G. Fichte thought it still necessary to put transcendental philosophy on secure foundations. The question that eventually emerges from this is not how we can tell who is really normal and who is really mad. The question, rather, is whether it is possible to distinguish normality from madness in a rigorous way at all.

Psychoanalysis began as an attempt to analyze patients diagnosed as being "abnormal" in some way. As he developed his theory, however, Freud came to wonder whether all subjects might be "abnormal" in some way. All subjects, he suggests, can be said to refuse to recognize a portion of reality. Some (neurotics) merely hide from reality; others (psychotics) invent an alternative reality (*SE* XIX, 183). Most people—so-called "normal" subjects—simply balance the degree to which they behave as neurotics or psychotics in this regard (*SE* XIX, 185).

Now suppose that we take both the neurotic refusal to recognize reality and the psychotic insistence on an alternative reality to correlate with judgments which a subject refuses to give up under any circumstances. We could then characterize these judgments as analytic in Quine's sense of the term. As judgments that purport to deny or reinvent reality, they are of course a posteriori judgments. Thus, it would turn out that every "normal" subject's web of beliefs would contain "abnormal" analytic a posteriori judgments. Here, of course, we would have to distinguish between "manifest" analytic a posteriori judgments which a subject would be aware of making, and "unconscious" analytic a posteriori judgments which do not enter consciousness. Why might such judgments remain repressed? Perhaps precisely so as to maintain their analytic character;

were the judgments to become conscious, they might be forced to submit to what Freud calls "reality testing."

As Lacan never tired of pointing out, the unconscious can be said to be structured like a language (e.g., Lacan 1977, 147; Lacan 1978, 203). My thesis is that this insight can be translated into Kantian terminology very simply: the unconscious is structured like a web of analytic a posteriori judgments.

In support of this claim, let me first acknowledge that Lacan's thesis concerns the connection not of judgments but of signifiers. If, however, we treat judgments primarily as links between concepts rather than as links between concepts and objects of intuition, and if we reduce the notion of a concept to that of a mere signifier, then this difference disappears. If, furthermore, we follow Quine in treating judgments not in isolation from one another but as existing in systematic relationship with one another, then a "web of beliefs" would turn out to be indistinguishable from a "network of signifiers." Like Lacan, Quine argues that language relates to the world only as a system. This system touches the world only at its edges: "The edge of the system must be kept squared with experience; the rest, with all its elaborate myths or fictions, has as its objective the simplicity of laws" (Quine 1980, 45).

Quine's distinction between the center and the periphery of the web of beliefs would more or less correspond to Freud's distinction between the thoughts of the unconscious and the thoughts of consciousness. Freud notes that the unconscious is characterized precisely by its unwillingness to give up its beliefs; this is what he means when he says that the unconscious acts as if it were both timeless and exempt from contradiction (*SE* XIV, 186–87). In a precisely analogous way, Quine refers to "our natural tendency to disturb the total system as little as possible" (Quine 1980, 44).

There are, of course, two crucial differences between the Quinean and psychoanalytic models. The first is that for Freud and Lacan (but not Quine) the core of this network is unconscious. Even here, however, we might note a parallel between Quine's claim that the web of beliefs touches the world only at or near its periphery and Freud's comparable claim that only some of the ideas in the preconscious can make their way into the field of consciousness. The second difference concerns Quine's claim that there are no analytic judgments. Here we could simply suppose that Quine's reluctance to recognize the existence of analytic (specifically analytic a posteriori) judgments is equivalent to his unwillingness to consider that the core of a web of beliefs might be exempt from reality testing altogether.

To say that the unconscious is the locus of analytic a posteriori judgments requires some topographical clarification. Because all judgments

—or signifying chains—are linked in some way to the analytic a posteriori judgments of the unconscious, these core judgments can be expected to exercise a kind of signifying effect on judgments located more at the periphery of the system. Accordingly, we might expect to find analytic a posteriori "effects" exhibited in consciousness (what I earlier called "manifest" analytic a posteriori judgments). Hence, I will distinguish between those analytic a posteriori judgments that appear in the unconscious and those that might appear as preconscious or conscious symptoms.

Perhaps the only difference between a "normal" subject and what Kant calls a "deranged" subject will be that all of the analytic a posteriori judgments of the "normal" subject remain unconscious, whereas those of the "deranged" subject are present in consciousness. To test this hypothesis, let us compare a supposedly "normal" metaphysician (Kant) to a supposedly "deranged" metaphysician.

In his *Memoirs of a Mental Illness*, Daniel Paul Schreber describes not only the details of his infirmity, but also the various theological discoveries he claims to have made while suffering from it. As such, the book is a full-blown attempt to outline a systematic theology, worthy of comparison with Kant's *Religion within the Limits of Reason*. As in the case of Kant's work, the heart of Schreber's theological treatise is the conception of moral duty which it contains: "God demands a *constant state of enjoyment*, such as would be in keeping with the conditions of existence imposed upon souls by the Order of Things; and it is my duty to provide Him with this" (cited in *SE* XII, 34). In his interpretation of Schreber's *Memoirs*, Freud himself notes that the text exhibits "as much ingenuity as every other theodicy" (*SE* XII, 28), and he promises to reveal to the reader the "method" in its "theologico-psychological system" (*SE* XII, 21).

Since Schreber's metaphysical judgments are in some way connected with his hallucinatory experiences, it makes sense to treat them as a posteriori rather than a priori. He suggests, moreover, that the truth of these judgments could not have been suspected a priori, for they fly in the face of precisely what would have been expected. Hence his constant expressions of surprise. He recalls, for instance, how shocked he was to discover that "*God really knew nothing about living men*" (Schreber's italics), a fact so unpredictable, so impossible to deduce a priori that "I myself feel inclined to exclaim: '*Incredible scriptu*!' " (*SE* XII, 25). He adds:

> The pen well-nigh shrinks from recording so monumental a piece of absurdity as that God, blinded by His ignorance of human nature, can positively go to such lengths as to suppose that there can exist a man too stupid to do what every animal can do—too stupid to be able to sh--. (*SE* XII, 27)

Given the a posteriori character of Schreber's judgment concerning the nature of his duty to God, one might suppose it is also a synthetic judgment. After all, in Kant's sense of the term, a judgment can be analytic only when the subject contains its predicate. Since we do not seem to find the predicate (providing a constant state of enjoyment) contained in the subject (the mere concept of duty), the judgment strikes us as incapable of being analytic. But perhaps this is just the point: *we* detect no analyticity in Schreber's delusional beliefs; perhaps, following Quine, we need to ask for whom a particular judgment would be analytic or synthetic. In the judgment, "My duty is to provide God with a constant state of enjoyment," the content of the subject ("my duty") remains obscure to us, so that we are simply not in a position to say whether *for Schreber* the judgment is ultimately analytic or synthetic. Experience has revealed to him, he says, that what God demands is itself necessitated by an "Order of Things." Perhaps this order of things establishes an analytic connection between the concept of duty and the concept of the demand of a constant state of enjoyment. Schreber's experience of this cosmic order might reveal to him the analyticity of a judgment whose truth, nonetheless, he could never have even discovered a priori.

Schreber insists upon the indubitability of his theological insights, even after acknowledging the delusional character of the experiences upon which they are based. During the time of his illness, apparently, he had come to believe that over two hundred years had expired, and that the world had come to an end only to be miraculously conjured up again. Later, presented with evidence that two hundred years had not elapsed, Schreber clings to his original belief *despite* recognizing the validity of the evidence against it. As Freud puts it:

> Years afterwards, when Dr. Schreber had returned to human society, and could find no trace in the books, the musical scores, or the other articles of daily use which fell into his hands once more, of anything to bear out his theory that there had been a gap of vast duration in the history of mankind, he admitted that his view was no longer tenable: ". . . I can no longer avoid recognizing that, *externally considered*, everything is as it used to be. *Whether, nevertheless, there may not have been a profound internal change* is a question to which I shall recur later." He could not bring himself to doubt that during his illness the world had come to an end and that, in spite of everything, the one that he now saw before him was a different one. (*SE* XII, 69)

It is as if, having climbed up the ladder of psychosis, he can now kick it away without having to come back down to earth.

Toward the end of his interpretation of the memoirs of Schreber—who, like Freud, poses as self-analyst, and who bequeaths to his interpreter the concept of a fundamental language (*Grundsprache*)—Freud notes the striking parallels between Schreber's delusions and his own metapsychological theory concerning these delusions. He adds: "It remains for the future to decide whether there is more delusion in my theory than I should like to admit, or whether there is more truth in Schreber's delusion than other people are as yet prepared to believe" (*SE* XII 79). I would alter the question only slightly by substituting for the name of Schreber the name of Kant. But ultimately, the similarities between Schreber and Kant are quite striking. For example, in a passage reminiscent of Schreber, Kant writes:

> I inevitably [*unausbleiblich*] believe in the existence of God and in a future life, and I am certain that nothing can shake this belief, since my moral principles would thereby be themselves overthrown [*umgestürzt*], and I cannot disclaim them without becoming abhorrent in my own eyes [*in meinen eigenen Augen verabscheuungswürdig*]. (A828/B856)

Freud says of Schreber, "he could not bring himself to doubt," thereby echoing Kant's claim that he cannot bring himself to doubt either. Kant, of course, would classify Schreber's judgment as springing from a deranged reason (Kant 1974, 85). But is there any rigorous way of distinguishing between these two metaphysical pronouncements?

Kant draws a distinction between dogmatic and critical metaphysical judgments. An example of the former can be found, for example, in the ontological argument; an example of the latter can be found in Kant's own moral justification for the necessity of believing in God. The understanding is said to overstep its boundaries whenever it takes concepts that have a proper immanent employment and applies them beyond the boundaries of possible experience, or whenever it invents fictitious concepts—Kant calls these "usurpatory concepts, such as *fortune, fate*" (A84/B117), which have no legitimate employment whatsoever—and applies these to objects of experience. Kant views the bad metaphysical statements that result from these illicit ways of thinking as easily corrected; as soon as a normal person becomes aware that he or she is making a mistake of this sort, he or she stops making the judgment immediately. On the other hand, the metaphysical illusions to which reason itself gives rise are good illusions (since they serve both a regulative and a moral function), and it is impossible to get rid of them (though it is necessary not to accept them dogmatically). Nonetheless, Kant wants to distinguish these illusions of reason from the delusions of a Schreber:

> In this last kind of mental derangement there is not merely lack of order and deviation from the rule for the use of reason, but also *positive unreason*: that is, *another* rule is present. The soul is transferred to a quite different standpoint, so to speak, and from it sees all objects differently. It is displaced from the *Sensorio communi* that is required for the unity of (animal) *life*, to a point far removed from it (hence the word *Verrückung*)—just as a mountainous landscape sketched from an aereal perspective calls forth a quite different judgment about the region than when it is viewed from the plain. It is true that the soul does not see or feel itself in another place (for it cannot perceive itself as situated in space without committing a contradiction, since it would then intuit itself as an object of its outer sense, whereas it can be only the object of inner sense); but this is how we account, as best we can, for the so-called displacement. (Kant 1974, 86)

In this fascinating passage, Kant obviously anticipates the metapsychological notion that the unconscious occurs in another place (*ein andere Schauplatz*). Kant both invokes and denies the possibility of the unconscious, since he claims that strictly speaking it is impossible for the subject to appear to itself as an object of outer sense. And yet this is precisely how Freud and Lacan interpret Schreber—the voice of God that he perceives as coming from outside him is nothing other than his own unconscious. I will take up in more detail the question of the relationship between the subject and outer sense in the next chapter. Here, however, I would stress that Kant insists that a "normal" subject is always centered in its own temporality; only a deranged subject would appear to be decentered.

But how are we to distinguish the stubbornness of delusion from the certainty of moral conviction? Schreber will not give up his belief. Kant also will not give up his belief. But, Kant says, I do not give up my belief because reason requires that I hold it, whereas Schreber does not give up his belief because he is a lunatic. Is this an argument?

It is noteworthy that Schreber seems willing to acknowledge the "madness" of his beliefs in a way that Kant does not recognize his. The perpetual astonishment to which Schreber gives expression might even be explained by supposing that he recognizes the analytic a posteriori character of his judgments. In other words, perhaps it is not the various "truths" about God which amaze him so but the fact that these "truths" are both analytically true and impossible to predict a priori. Yes, he freely admits, these judgments are all based on experience; how much more amazing, he concludes, that they are necessary! Schreber's astonishment would be that of the good Quinean who is shocked to discover that he holds certain a posteriori beliefs to be analytic after all. Like the character in Voltaire who suddenly realizes he has been speaking prose all his life, Schreber's discovery would represent a genuine insight of sorts—one not shared by Kant.

In short, the difference between Kant and Schreber would be that Schreber understands his symptoms in a way that Kant does not understand his. Nonetheless, analytic a posteriori judgments appear as manifest symptoms in Kant just as much as they do in Schreber. This is not to say that every web of beliefs must contain manifest analytic a posteriori judgments. It is possible to imagine subjects whose webs of beliefs would contain no such manifest judgments, but which nonetheless contain analytic a posteriori judgments at the level of the unconscious. This could be the case in hysteria—for reasons I will take up in the next chapter.

But there is also a topographical question to consider here. Analytic a posteriori judgments that appear in consciousness could be said to have arrived there by either of two routes. On the one hand, they could be formed on the basis of perceptions of which the subject is immediately conscious—in which case they might first have been formed as synthetic judgments. On the other hand, they could arise from the unconscious—in which case they would be analytic "on arrival" as it were. I will call the former "material" and the latter "formal" manifest analytic a posteriori judgments. The chief difference would be that material analytic a posteriori judgments would take what are at first contingently connected empirical signifiers and make their connection necessary; formal analytic a posteriori judgments would begin as necessary connections in the unconscious before rising to the level of consciousness.

To illustrate, a jealous husband could be someone who forms material analytic a posteriori judgments. Thus, according to Freud, a husband might first perceive minor signs of his wife's unfaithfulness and then obsessively turn the contingent connection between his idea of his wife and his idea of her unfaithfulness into a necessary connection (*SE* XVIII, 226). By contrast, Schreber's belief that God demands a constant state of enjoyment might be a connection that appears in his consciousness as necessary (i.e., analytic) from the start.

This distinction recalls Kripke's contrast between the "necessary a posteriori" and the "contingent a priori." Kripke's distinction contrasts two different ways in which something can be known to be true. Since it is possible to learn a necessary truth by way of experience, he claims, it must be possible that there are necessary a posteriori truths. "Something may belong in the realm of such statements that *can* be known *a priori* but still may be known by particular people on the basis of experience" (Kripke 1980, 35). In one way, Kripke's necessary a posteriori knowledge might seem to correlate with what I am calling the material analytic a posteriori. Of course, in the latter case, the subject has not learned a necessary truth by way of experience; rather, he or she has formulated an analytic judgment on the basis of what were originally contingently connected concepts or signifiers.

Kripke further suggests that if naming is understood as rigid designation, it will turn out that there are contingent truths about particular named things which ought nonetheless to be called a priori truths. To the extent that experience here gives rise to judgments the truth of which requires no appeal to experience we might compare Kripke's contingent a priori to what I am calling the formal analytic a posteriori. But again, in the latter case, the subject has not established a truth by rigidly fixing the reference of an object; rather, his or her web of beliefs contains an empirical judgment whose imagined validity requires the seeking-out of a rigidly defined object (as in the case of anti-Semitism, so brilliantly analyzed by Žižek). Of course, in either case, the analyticity of a judgment will entail beliefs against which no counterfactual evidence can count. Take, for example, a paranoid subject's belief that a particular person is trying to kill him. The analyticity of this judgment is such that the subject will believe that this person is trying to kill him even, so to speak, in those possible worlds in which this person does not exist; or, more precisely, there can be no worlds in which "this person" does not exist, since someone can always be made to fill the marker. Similarly, Freud suggests that a jealous husband who is obsessed with the idea that his wife is cheating on him can be described as paranoid even if it turns out that his wife *is* cheating on him (*SE* XVIII, 226).

Both the necessary a posteriori and the contingent a priori are ways of classifying knowledge about the world, whereas the material and formal analytic a posteriori refer not to types of knowledge but to what we might call epistemic symptoms. That Kripke's theory is more concerned with truths than with beliefs is connected with his aim of treating all questions of identity as ontological issues rather than as epistemological issues. Whatever the other merits of this approach, it suffers from the same drawback that every attempt to place a theory of reference before a theory of signification does—it assumes that meaning is a function of reference. But even shifting from an ontological perspective to an epistemological one, as for example Palmquist suggests, would not solve matters either. The problem posed by metapsychology requires a shift from questions concerning truth and knowledge to questions concerning the nature and causes of judgment. That Kripke overlooks such questions is evidenced by the fact that he takes for granted his belief that it is possible to name something. By contrast, someone like Hume—precisely as a thinker of the analytic a posteriori—takes the question of the nature and causes of judgment to be his principal concern. In the end, not surprisingly, Hume is led to wonder whether naming is possible at all—both in the case of indexicals intended to pick out objects of perception and in the case of the indexical "I."

When Kant tries to explain the possibility of the synthetic a priori, he poses the question as follows: "What is here the unknown = X which gives support to the understanding when it believes that it can discover outside the concept A a predicate B foreign to this concept, which it yet at the same time considers to be connected with it?" (A9/B13). Parallel to Kant, the question to be considered here is: "What is here the unknown = X which incites the understanding to connect contingently connected signifiers in an analytic way?"

But this question points to an enigma concerning that which would "cause" the understanding to form an analytic a posteriori judgment. To invoke the term "cause" here would be precipitous. Kant notes that we cannot inquire into that which is the cause of the transcendental (nor can we ask if things in themselves might be the causes of the sensory manifold) without losing all sense of what we could possibly mean by the concept of causality. Just as he will define the transcendental object merely as an "X" about which we can say nothing intelligible, so there might be nothing intelligible about that "X" which "causes" the understanding to make analytic a posteriori judgments. Because the questions posed by metapsychology will concern the conditions for the possibility of the Kantian categories of the understanding, it would be question-begging to invoke the concept of causality in raising such questions. For this reason, I have used the word "incites" in place of the word "causes," asking what "incites" the understanding to posit the analytic a posteriori. Strictly speaking, of course, the word "incites" is no better than the word "causes" unless we keep in mind that the meaning of "incites" must be left obscure. In general, the language of metapsychology will be obscure in this very precise sense. Nicolas Abraham indicates what is at stake here, invoking the term *anasemia* to refer to the indeterminate skewing of language carried out by metapsychology:

> Let us take any term introduced by Freud, whether he coined it or simply borrowed it from scientific or colloquial language. Unless one is deaf to their meaning, one is struck, as soon as Freudian terms are related to the unconscious Kernel, by the vigor with which they literally rip themselves away from the dictionary and ordinary language. The allusion to the nonreflexive and the unnamed in fact induces this unprecedented and strange semantic phenomenon. The language of psychoanalysis no longer

> follows the twists and turns (*tropoi*) of customary speech and writing. Pleasure, Id, Ego, Economic, Dynamic, are not metaphors, metonymies, synecdoches, catachreses; they are, by dint of discourse, products of designification and constitute new figures, absent from rhetorical treatises. These figures of antisemantics, inasmuch as they signify no more than the action of moving up toward the source of their customary meaning, require a denomination properly indicative of their status and which—for want of something better—I shall propose to designate by the neologism *anasemia.* (Abraham and Torok 1994, 85)

Later, I will use the word *drive* (*Trieb, pulsion*) in order to refer to that which "incites" the understanding, on the assumption that this term can also function only anasemically.

In keeping with the plan of a point by point antithetic to the first *Critique*, there are three overarching sets of questions to consider: whether and how analytic a posteriori judgments are possible in: (1) mathematics, (2) science, and (3) metaphysics. But the parallelism in structure also requires an inversion in method. For Kant, the synthetic a priori reveals the existence of pure conditions of possible experience. To view the synthetic a priori as analytic a posteriori is, on the contrary, to seek the empirical wherever reason purports to find the pure. This is the shared strategy of Hume, Freud, and Lacan. What will emerge from an antithetic to the Kantian project, accordingly, will be not transcendental conditions for possible experience but *symptomatic structures*, specifically: (1) neuroses, (2) perversions, and (3) psychoses.

2

# Aesthetics of Neurosis

> Nothing is more apparent to the senses, than the distinction betwixt a curve and a right line; nor are there any ideas we more easily form than the ideas of these objects. But however easily we may form these ideas, 'tis impossible to produce any definition of them, which will fix the precise boundaries betwixt them.
> —Hume 1978, 49

> The sinuous line inscribes the chain which permits a calculus of the subject. It is directed, and its direction constitutes an order in which the appearance of the *objet a* in the place of the cause is made clear by the universality of its relation to the category of causality, which, in forcing the threshold of Kant's transcendental deduction, would inaugurate a new Critique of Reason hinging upon the impure.
> —Lacan 1989, 63

Why is the secret of neurosis to be sought in mathematics?

According to Freud, the neuroses in general result when the ego represses an instinctual impulse originating in the id (*SE* XIX, 149–50). Because of this repression, the impulse remains or becomes unconscious, finding its way back into consciousness only through a symptom. To put this in Kantian terms, we could say that repression deflects something away from the understanding and on to sensibility. As an object of sensible but not intellectual intuition, the significance of the symptom would remain hidden; qua spatial or temporal object of intuition, it would be on the side of sensibility rather than the side of understanding. Yet insofar as every object of intuition appears, as it were, before the tribunal of the understanding, the appearance of the symptom would mark a kind of return of the repressed.

Here, however, we see the return of the repressed leading to a split within the understanding, akin to Freud's notion of the splitting of the ego. As an object of intuition, the neurotic symptom is something that calls forth judgment; however, as an appearance in nature whose significance remains hidden, the neurotic symptom is something that cannot be judged. This split corresponds to Kant's division between the mathematical categories and the dynamical categories. The mathematical categories (quantity and quality) are applicable to everything in intuition; the dynamical categories (relation and modality) are applicable to appearances only insofar as these exist in systematic connection with each other in nature. For Freud, the neurotic will be conscious of *having* a symptom (i.e., can apply categories of quantity and quality to it) but will be unable to *explain* it—i.e., will be unable to reconstruct a "dynamical" narrative that will situate the symptom in its place in the order of causes. This suggests that both "in itself" and "for the subject" in question, neurotic symptoms can be classified as mathematical rather than dynamical.

Lacan's theory of the genesis of subjectivity requires two stages. The first of these is the mirror stage, when the subject first appears solely as a "geometrical" subject, identified with a visual object of outer intuition. In this original misapprehension (*méconnaissance*), Lacan locates both the origin of "geometrical" representations of space, and the fact that the subject first appears on the side of the Other (Lacan 1977, 27).

After the mirror stage, the subject's unconscious begins to develop out of the auditory data of heard discourse: "The unconscious is constituted by [*ce sont*] the effects of speech on the subject" (Lacan 1978, 149). This process coincides with the formation of the subject's ego and ego ideal. We can think of it as the "echo stage," for unlike the visual and geometrical imago with which the mirror stage subject identifies, the auditory subject of the echo stage identifies with purely temporal objects (heard sounds). Just as the mirror imago is constituted in the gaze of the Other, so the echo fixation is constituted, as it were, in the voice of the Other.

Hence, the spatial subject is older than the temporal subject, which implies a profound inversion of the Kantian model. Although in his narrative Kant presents an analysis of space before his analysis of time, he eventually identifies the subject of intuition with the temporal subject. Thus, according to Kant, all of the subject's representations take place in time; only some represent objects in space:

> Time is the formal *a priori* condition of all appearances whatsoever. Space, as the pure form of all *outer* intuition, is so far limited; it serves as the *a priori* condition only of outer appearances. But since all representations, whether they have for their object outer things or not, belong, in themselves, as determinations of the mind, to our inner state; and since this inner state stands under the formal condition of inner intuition, and so belongs to time, time is an *a priori* condition of all appearance whatsoever. (A34/B50)

For Lacan, by contrast, it would turn out that all representations take place in space; only some would represent objects in time. This is because the time of the subject of the echo stage is already situated in the geometrical field in which the subject is identified with its mirror imago. It is for this reason that the unconscious exists, according to Lacan, in the locus of the Other: it exists in the geometrical field of space.

We can use the distinction between the subject of space and the subject of time to elucidate the difference between hysteria and obsessional neurosis. Hysteria manifests itself in symptoms that are spatial in character; thus they exhibit geometrical structures. Obsessional neurosis manifests itself in symptoms that are temporal in character; thus they exhibit arithmetical structures. Or, to put the point in more strictly Kantian terms, hysterical symptoms will appear on the subject's body qua object of outer sense; obsessional symptoms will appear in the subject's body qua object of inner sense.

It also follows that hysterical symptoms would mark a regression to the mirror stage; obsessional symptoms would mark a regression to the echo stage. The hysteric is defined as being caught in a geometrical identification with the Other, unable to count himself or herself as a subject who "counts." Put otherwise, the hysterical subject regresses to the level of a pre-arithmetical subject who can situate himself or herself only within a signifying space whose objectively given geometrical structure precludes the perspectival view of the consciously perceiving subject who will do geometry by "counting" (the Cartesian coordinate system). This is why Freud suggests that hysterics "act out" rather than remember their repressed fantasies—and here it would be worth recalling that the German word for remembering—*Erinnerung*—suggests precisely a "making inward" (which the hysteric does not do) (*SE* VII, 119).

By contrast, the obsessional neurotic would regress to the level of arithmetical judgment. However, just as the hysterical subject would be "pre-arithmetical," so the obsessional caught at the level of the arithmetical would act as if he or she were a "pregeometrical" subject. This would explain why Kant, for example, restricts the subject's empirical manifestation to a temporal dimension. But if the arithmetical subject must already have passed through the mirror stage, how are we to account for the obsessional's appearance of being "pregeometrical"? Perhaps we could answer this question in terms of Freud's appeal to the "loss of reality" that takes place no less in neurosis than it does in psychosis (*SE* XIX, 183). The problem with this suggestion is that neurosis in general seems to imply only a partial break with objects of outer intuition, whereas the obsessional subject is completely nongeometrical. But what if undergoing the echo stage required a temporary suspension of the identification with the mirror imago? Only after having passed through the echo stage would the subject identify its ego and ego ideal with its mirror imago. Then it would not be surprising to find the obsessional's regression to the echo stage characterized by a suspension of the geometrical.

The obsessional subject is characterized by having a strong superego and, as such, the obsessional's fundamental experience is of being judged. At the level of consciousness, the obsessional appears to itself as a judging subject, but this is because it is identified with the voices that judge it; at the level of unconscious guilt, the obsessional is a judged subject. Thus, in his essay "Kant with Sade," Lacan contends that the Kantian subject simply fails to recognize that the moral law does not spring from within but is imposed on it from the field of the Other.

Since, for Lacan, the subject is what one signifier represents for another signifier (see, e.g. Lacan 1978, 67), language will not be something that belongs to the subject as an ability or faculty that it possesses; rather, its subjectivity will be an effect of language. Translating into Kantian terms, this will mean that the subject does not "possess" a faculty of judgment; the subject is something represented by judgments. For this reason, metapsychology does not interrogate the power of subjects to judge but rather the ability of judgments to conjure an "I think" that can always be attached to them.

At its most basic level, a network of signifiers is to be explained as a system of combinatorial possibilities. If, then, the judging subject is an effect of a network of signifiers, this suggests that the judging subject will appear as an effect of combination—i.e., as an effect of *counting*:

> The important thing, for us, is that we are seeking here—before any formation of the subject, of a subject who thinks, who situates himself in it—the level at which there is counting [*ça compte*], things are counted, and in this counting he who counts is already included. (Lacan 1978, 20)

The subject who eventually appears to itself qua judging subject will be an arithmetical subject-who-can-count. But the subject-who-can-count will itself be the effect of a counting that has constituted it. Lacan illustrates with the example of someone who says, "*I have three brothers, Paul, Ernest and me*" (Lacan 1978, 20). This, he suggests, gives an accurate reconstruction of the logic whereby first the structural field exists as counted up (three brothers) and then the counting subject (me) appears.

For Lacan, then, to be a symbolic subject is to be a counted/counting subject—in precisely the same way that for Kant to be a human subject is to be capable of doing arithmetic: "It is at this level, not of the one, but of the *one* one, at the level of the reckoning [*du compte*], that the subject has to situate himself as such" (Lacan 1978, 141). The connection between subjectivity and counting recalls Kant's argument that arithmetic is the vehicle through which a subject is capable of representing its inner intuition of itself. But strictly speaking, the Lacanian subject is not counter but counted; it is the *object* of arithmetical judgment. The ability to count will seem to the counting subject to be a synthetic a priori capacity which it possesses only until it discovers that it is not the agent but the effect of counting. According to Kant, time is an a priori form of inner intuition, and arithmetic—counting—is made possible by virtue of the fact that time is a pure form of intuition. But if Lacan is right, then strictly speaking counting will take place prior to the appearance of both the subject of inner intuition and of time itself.

The subject who takes itself to count would be, as I have suggested, the subject of an obsessional neurosis; of the Rat Man Freud notes, "Another time, as they were sitting together during a thunderstorm, he was obsessed, he could not tell why, with the *necessity for counting* up to forty or fifty between each flash of lightning and its accompanying thunderclap" (*SE* X, 189–90). It is easy to see in the temporal regimentation of obsessional neurosis in general a kind of compulsive counting. That such symptoms would be strictly arithmetical but not geometrical would be suggested by the fact that the obsessional neurotic does not *enact* the fantasies to which he or she is tempted: "these impulses never—literally never—force their way through to performance; the outcome lies always in victory for the flight and the precautions" (*SE* XVI, 259). By avoiding bodily enactments—or by engaging only in those that can be arithmeticized—the obsessional neurotic avoids the geometrical schematizing of its impulses. Through perpetual deferral rather than enactment, the obsessional's symptom of pure temporalization is established.

In the case of both hysteria and obsessional neurosis, the subject which appears to itself as capable of making synthetic a priori judgments would be the effect of preexisting analytic a posteriori judgments. In the previous chapter, I suggested that hysterics might exhibit no manifest analytic a posteriori judgments, whereas obsessional neurotics would. Why should this be the case?

Suppose we take Freud's contrasting cases of Dora and the Rat Man. In his interpretation of Dora, Freud focuses on dreams rather than on conscious thoughts, precisely because he assumes that there are no manifest analytic a posteriori judgments in Dora's symptoms. Thus, he says that women like Dora, unlike obsessional neurotics, "are entirely without insight into their illness" (*SE* VII, 20). By contrast, in his "Notes upon a Case of Obsessional Neurosis," Freud shows that the conscious life of the Rat Man was fraught with analytic a posteriori symptoms.

He would regularly formulate such judgments as "If I marry the lady, some misfortune will befall my father," and "*If you indulge in intercourse, something will happen to Ella*" (*SE* X, 226). Freud's interpretive procedure is to trace these judgments back to the unconscious analytic a posteriori judgments from which they derive (though of course he does not quite put it that way).

The Rat Man's judgments are all temporal in character. In each case, there is a fear of enactment articulated as the temporal threat that something will happen in the future as a result of the action. In fact, it is precisely in order to ward off the threat of enactment that his analytic a posteriori judgments force themselves to the level of consciousness with all the insistence of the drive. By contrast, Dora's difficulty is not with enactment (as Freud seems to think) but with becoming, so to speak, a subject-who-counts. For this reason, Dora's repression—her not having judgments that rise to the level of consciousness—is precisely the core of her hysteria. In other words, it is not the content of particular repressed judgments that is refused from consciousness; it is the mere fact of these judgments that is kept at the level of her geometrical identifications with the Other.

To treat space and time as effects of analytic a posteriori formations, as Lacan does, is to explicate the possibility of mathematical judgment in preintuitive terms. Anticipations of Lacan's approach can be found in Hume, for whom there is no such thing as a Kantian form of intuition. Thus, in the *Treatise,* the very ideas of space and time are said to derive from a prior discursivity—notably, the automatic way in which contiguous impressions are associated with each other.

It is important to stress that, for Hume, the association of contiguous impressions is not dependent on any deliberate act of the conscious subject. Moreover, the idea of contiguity does not presuppose the ideas of either spatiality or temporality. Things work, rather, the other way around—whatever ideas of space and time emerge in consciousness are derived from the automatic association of contiguous impressions. The ideas of space and time are simply copies of the ideas of contiguous tactile or visual impressions. Thus, the mathematician's supposed idea of empty space—the idea of a vacuum—is not a presupposition of geometry but merely a confused result of empirical geometrical reasoning taken to an inconclusive extreme. It is only because the mind is capable of making judgments about the contiguity of colored and tactile points that it imagines it possesses an idea of empty space. Thus, far from mathematical discursivity being grounded in a pure idea of space, there is for Hume—following Berkeley—no clear and distinct idea of pure space (or time) whatsoever. The illusion that we possess innate forms of intuition must therefore be grounded in the possibility of mathematical discursivity rather than the other way around.

Hume's point could be restated as follows. All mathematical judgments are a posteriori, but the mind has a habit of treating them as if they were analytic as well. Take the judgment that a straight line (or, as Hume says, a "right line") "*is the shortest way betwixt two points*" (Hume 1978, 49–50). According to Hume, mathematicians deceive themselves when they say that this is a definition (Hume 1978, 49). Strictly speaking, the statement should be treated as an empirical hypothesis to be demonstrated rather than as a stipulative definition, for prior to experience there is no reason to suppose that the idea of a straight line should entail the thought of its being the shortest way between two points (Hume 1978, 50). Kant, of course, would say that this proves that the judgment in question is synthetic. Hume could agree, but would maintain that there is no pure idea of space that could make the judgment a priori. Since the judgment is not a priori but is rather a posteriori, the only way to explain the sense of necessity we have concerning the judgment is to conclude that it is supported by unconscious judgments: *the mind has already formed analytic a posteriori connections among contiguous impressions.*

The illusion that we possess an idea of pure space is traced, then, to a symptom—the fact that the mind has a tendency to produce what I am calling material analytic a posteriori judgments. Noting the illegitimacy of such judgments, Hume concludes that they must arise because of deeper structures over which the subject has no control.

The idea that the subject might not be in control of its mathematical judgments is one that Kant refuses. At least since Descartes, however, the problematic of madness has regularly been associated with the possibility that one might persistently make mathematical mistakes without realizing it. Descartes worries about this in his First Meditation. Prior to the appeal to the *cogito* as an independent standard of rational self-knowledge, he contends, there is no way to establish certainty even about simple mathematical judgments:

> Moreover, since I judge that others sometimes make mistakes in matters that they believe they know most perfectly, may I not, in like fashion, be deceived every time I add two and three or count the sides of a square, or perform an even simpler operation, if that can be imagined? (Descartes 1993, 15)

Despite the fact that he will subsequently establish the possibility of a mathematicization of knowledge, Descartes here maintains that the subject's claim to self-mastery cannot be deduced from its mathematical certainty; on the contrary, mathematical certainty depends on an independent solution to the problem of the madness of the critical subject. Descartes is therefore forced to shift from grounding the rationality of the critical subject in the certainty of mathematical knowledge to grounding mathematical knowledge in the *cogito*'s independent certainty of its own existence. And—as Lacan shows—it is only with the appeal to the Other in the Third Meditation that Descartes reestablishes the possibility of mathematical certainty:

> I can do no more than suggest the extraordinary consequences that have stemmed from this handing back of truth into the hands of the Other, in this instance the perfect God, whose truth is the nub of the matter, since, whatever he might have meant, would always *be* the truth—even if he had said that two and two make five, it would have been true. (Lacan 1978, 36)

Kant, however, cannot go this route, for he argues that the *cogito* is unable to guarantee any knowledge concerning either the question of its ultimate nature or of the question of God's existence. Instead of providing an alternative answer to the problem of madness raised by Descartes, Kant simply assumes that mathematical certainty cannot be called into question. Thus the *Critique* takes it for granted that mathematics is a "sound [*gründlicher*] science . . . which rest[s] upon a secure foundation [*deren Grund gut gelegt ist*]" (Axii). The only question, as far as Kant is concerned, is how we are to explain the *fact* of mathematical certainty. It is this dogmatic assumption alone—one which Descartes himself challenges—that allows Kant to maintain that arithmetical and geometrical judgments must be a priori (B14).

It is for this reason alone that Kant expects little argument as to the a prioricity of mathematical judgments. He presumes that the burden of his argument is to show that such judgments cannot be derived from concepts alone and so must be synthetic:

> Geometrical propositions, that, for instance, in a triangle two sides together are greater than the third, can never be derived from the general concepts of line and triangle, but only from intuition, and this indeed *a priori,* with apodeictic certainty. (A25/B39)

The distinction between intuitions and concepts is of course crucial for Kant. He criticizes the empiricists for sensualizing concepts and the rationalists for intellectualizing appearances (A271/B327). But in order to maintain a sharp division here, Kant runs into difficulties. For the schemata of the categories to be possible at all, the gap between concepts and appearances cannot be as great as Kant would make it out to be. Otherwise, how could we account for the fact that the schemata are themselves both sensible and intellectual? (A138/B177). When pressed, Kant seems prepared to declare that the schemata are themselves concepts, particularly when he attempts to distinguish judgments based on the construction of mathematical concepts from transcendental propositions. Whereas mathematical judgments require an appeal to intuitions, Kant argues, transcendental propositions are merely discursive:

> With the concept of cause I do really go beyond the empirical concept of an event (something happening), yet I do not pass to the intuition which exhibits the concept of cause *in concreto*, but to the time-conditions in general, which in experience may be found to be in accord with this concept. I therefore proceed merely in accordance with concepts; I cannot proceed by means of the construction of concepts, since the concept is a rule of the synthesis of perceptions, and the latter are not pure intuitions, and so do not permit of being *given a priori*. (A722/B750)

This passage underscores the fact that the categories are rules for the synthesis of empirical perceptions; they do not yield intuitions per se. In referring to particular time-conditions (*Zeitbedingungen*), the schemata remain at the level of the *concept* of time. Their merely discursive character suggests that their role as mediators of concepts and intuitions is more complicated than that of a simple linking of concepts and intuitions. Kant claims that transcendental propositions in general do not unite concepts and intuitions in the way that mathematical propositions do:

> A transcendental proposition is therefore synthetic knowledge through reason, in accordance with mere concepts; and it is discursive, in that while it is what alone makes possible any synthetic unity of empirical knowledge, it yet gives us no intuition *a priori*. (A722/B750)
>
> Philosophy confines itself to universal concepts; mathematics can achieve nothing by concepts alone but hastens at once to intuition, in which it considers the concept *in concreto*. (A715/B743)

Critics of Kant have frequently argued that the appeal to something other than concepts is not necessary in mathematics. In Kant's day, so a familiar story goes, it might have seemed plausible to think that something like the parallel postulate could be demonstrated only by appeal to intuition, but the later development of non-Euclidean geometries showed that it is possible to "do" mathematics without relating one's manipulations of concepts or signifiers to intuition. As long as these geometries were merely tools of mathematicians, Kant's defenders could note that they had no possible applicability to experience. However, Einstein's theory of general relativity refuted this supposition rather decisively.

What this story tends to overlook is the fact that Kant does not deny that it is possible to relate concepts to one another without showing how they could be applied to experience. What he claims is that we can have no idea of what such judgments would *mean.* It is true that he rejects the possibility of there being any knowledge which violates the limits that are given by the Euclidean forms of intuition and by the categories, and that he limits mathematical knowledge to the construction of concepts of intuition. But, presumably, Kant could acknowledge the possibility of non-Euclidean discursive mathematics as a consistent body of judgments; he would simply deny the meaningfulness—and therefore the truth-value—of such judgments.

It seems to me there are some advantages for Lacanian theory in accepting this view. If we treat the purely discursive dimension of concepts as the order of the signifier and intuition as the field of the signified, Kant's point could be restated by noting that symbolic meaning and the order of truth are constituted only through a falling of the signifier into the signified. For Lacan, modern mathematics consists solely of the manipulation of meaningless signifiers. However, unlike Wittgenstein, for whom the question of the meaning of mathematics drops out altogether, Lacan preserves the question of meaning at the level of the subject. That is, the meaning of a mathematical judgment is given in the subject that appears as its "schematized" effect in the field of intuition.

On Kant's view, concepts become meaningful only insofar as they are applied to intuitions: "We therefore demand that a bare [*abgesonderten*] concept be *made sensible,* that is, that an object corresponding to it be presented in intuition. Otherwise the concept would, as we say, be without *sense,* that is, without meaning" (A240/B299). However, Kant's theory of meaning is complicated by his invocation of the phenomena/noumena distinction. By retaining the notion of the thing in itself, and by allowing that concepts which are not applicable to any possible experience might nonetheless be deemed problematic with respect to the noumena, Kant acknowledges that there can be judgments which, though not meaningful, are not simply meaningless either. This is one of the many places where Kant makes use of the logical function of the infinite judgment. In effect, judgments about things in themselves are classified as "nonmeaningful," which is not the same as "meaningless." Keeping this distinction in mind, we might think of pure mathematics as consisting of nonmeaningful statements which can become meaningful only through something like a schematization of intuitions.

For example, we could say that Euclidean geometry "makes sense" to us simply because we have a way of exhibiting some of its propositions in intuition. Riemannian geometry became meaningful when Einstein schematized it with the general theory of relativity. Of course, the theory of relativity does not represent the only possible schemata for Riemannian geometry, just as there is no reason why a particular set of contiguous colored dots on a piece of paper should represent the only possible schema for the concept of a straight line. The concept of a straight line can be schematized in very different ways; the schema of a straight line in a set of blueprints is not the same as the schema of a straight line in a perspective drawing. Lacan brings out some of the implications of this in his discussion of anamorphosis (Lacan 1978, 92).

To return to the case of arithmetic, consider once again the judgment "7 + 5 = 12." Taken by itself, this judgment is implied by—and in turn implies—an indefinitely large body of judgments concerning the concept of number. What exactly it might mean we could never say if we had not some schematized experience of what counting is. Yet the experience of counting is not a necessary precondition for learning the rules of arithmetic, any more than possession of the faculty of hearing is necessary for learning how to play the piano from a musical score. The ascription of something like meaning to a system of musical notation is not a prerequisite for learning how the signifiers of this system are manipulated (for instance, in the transposition of a piece from one key to another). In the case of counting, the subject learns the system while simultaneously having the various judgments schematized for it; that is, one counts with the Other one's fingers, toes, etc.

Because we learn to count by learning the schemata of counting, we are led to view the meaning—and ourselves—as being "already there" in the combination of signifiers that counting is. In this way, we are led to the mistaken view that the meaning of mathematical judgments is given a priori. From this, of course, it would seem to follow that the appeal to the experience of actual counting must be superfluous; yet at the same time the intrinsically nonmeaningful character of the judgment itself seems to show that some appeal to intuition must be necessary to give it meaning. Kant solves this dilemma by distinguishing between pure and empirical intuitions: the pure forms of intuition must be posited as the support which alone could give a nonmeaningful judgment its meaning in an a priori way. However, it is clear that the distinction between pure and empirical intuition arises only if we fail to recognize that what count as forms of intuition are themselves the products of schemata. The tendency to posit pure transcendental limits simply arises from the confusion of the analytic a posteriori with the synthetic a priori. It is not because time appears the way it does that 7 + 5 = 12; rather, it is because 7 + 5 = 12 that time appears the way it does. Why does 7 + 5 = 12? As Lacan suggests with respect to the Cartesian God who could have made it true that 2 + 2 = 5, such a question is not irrelevant from a metapsychological perspective.

Before returning to Lacan's treatment of the relation between arithmetic and the counted/counting subject, I want to look at Freud's attempt to speculate on the origin of the ideas of space and time. Freud asks us to imagine "a living organism in its most simplified possible form," with a surface that is "turned towards the external world," and from which it receives stimuli. Over time, he postulates, this surface would be so bombarded with stimuli that its outermost layer would "become permanently modified." Specifically: "a crust would thus be formed which would at last have been so thoroughly 'baked through' by stimulation that it would present the most favourable possible conditions for the reception of stimuli and become incapable of any further modification" (*SE* XVIII, 26). The process whereby this outer crust is formed represents, for Freud, a model for explaining how it is that human perception comes to be structured by certain limiting conditions of experience. But the explanation requires a further positing of a dynamical relationship between the rest of the organism and its baked-over crust. Freud speculates that this crust functions more as a protective shield against stimuli than it does as a vehicle for the reception of stimuli (*SE* XVIII, 27). He then proposes that perception takes place when the sense organs of the organism go out like "feelers" and "sample" the stimuli that are bombarding the protective shield (*SE* XVIII, 28).

Having presented this speculative model, Freud uses it as a basis for explaining "the Kantian theorem that time and space are 'necessary forms of thought' " (*SE* XVIII, 28). First, the cyclical process whereby the sense-organs send out and withdraw their feelers can be viewed as giving rise to the idea of time which the organism possesses. In "A Note upon the 'Mystic Writing-Pad,' " Freud suggests that it is "this discontinuous method of functioning" which "lies at the bottom of the origin of the concept of time" (*SE* XIX, 231). As for the origin of the idea of space, Freud draws on a distinction between internal and external sources of excitations from stimuli. The outer crust protects the organism from external stimuli only, not from internal stimuli. The only way for the organism to protect itself against the painful excitations of internal stimuli is, at first, through *projection*, positing their source as existing outside of itself in space. (A similar explanation of the phenomenon of projection can already be found in Nietzsche.) Freud is more explicit in a short note written in 1938: "Space may be the projection of the extension of the psychical apparatus. No other derivation is probable. Instead of Kant's *a priori* determinants of our psychical apparatus" (*SE* XXIII, 300). Thus, it is not the mere recognition of an external stimulus as external that occasions the idea of space, but the projection of an internal stimulus as external; like Kant, Freud here implicitly assumes a distinction between the mere possession of a discursive concept of the outer and the idea of spatiality per se.

At the heart of Freud's encrustation model is the hypothesis that stimuli are painful—although strictly speaking the theory of eros developed in *Beyond the Pleasure Principle* complicates this picture. The ideas of time and space would be inventions born of an organism's desire to avoid painful excitations: temporal rhythms would keep external sources of pain at bay, and spatial projection would attempt to put internal sources of pain out of reach.

Freud's emphasis is on the origin of the distinction between inner and outer; presumably, he takes the more sophisticated possibilities of arithmetic and Euclidean geometry to follow as later consequences. This is why Lacan could be said to take Freud's problematic one step further back. In his essay on the mirror stage, Lacan begins by reporting the empirical observation that an infant of a certain age delights in seeing its image in the mirror (Lacan 1977, 1). At this point in its development, the infant does not possess motor control and has not as yet developed an idea of itself as ego. Much as Hegel, in the *Phenomenology*, presents the earliest form of experience as mere consciousness, so Lacan presumes that at this early point in its life, an infant will be absorbed in that which it perceives. The question is how it is that the infant comes to distinguish between itself and the world and in this way arrive at an idea of the difference "between the *Innenwelt* and the *Umwelt*" (Lacan 1977, 4). Lacan answers this question by supposing that the infant's first idea of itself is an idea of a projected spatial representation with which it identifies; Lacan invokes the psychoanalytic concept of an "imago" (Lacan 1977, 2). The imago represents for the infant an *anticipation* of itself as subject. By identifying itself with the imago, the infant posits itself as something it is not yet:

> The *mirror stage* is a drama whose internal thrust [*poussée*] is precipitated from insufficiency to anticipation—and which manufactures for the subject, caught up in the lure of spatial identification, the succession of phantasies that extends from a fragmented body-image to a form of its totality that I shall call orthopaedic—and, lastly, to the assumption of the armour of an alienating identity, which will mark with its rigid structure the subject's entire mental development. Thus, to break out of the circle of the *Innenwelt* into the *Umwelt* generates the inexhaustible quadrature of the ego's verifications [*récolements*]. (Lacan 1977, 4)

Presumably, the word *armour* (*l'armure*) here corresponds to what Freud takes to be the "crust." But Lacan's theory adds a new twist. Because the distinction between inner and outer, self and world, is constituted through an identification with something outer (the mirror image), the identity of what will later be the "inner" subject appears, at first, where it is not.

Here we find the elementary matrix of Lacan's famous formula that "the subject is what one signifier represents for another signifier." On Lacan's reading, the imago with which the infant identifies is a sort of "*Ur*-signifier." "Identification," of course, has to be understood not in the sense of an already constituted "I" identifying with something else, but in the sense of a movement which constitutes the "I" as something always already identified with its other.

Lacan's theory, arguably just as speculative as Freud's, suggests that the distinction between inner and outer can never be rigorously drawn; it is always "a question of something inside that is also outside" (Lacan 1978, 147). Moreover, the theory emphasizes the contingency of where it is that the eventual subject will divide itself from the world—a point to which I will return. Finally, the theory locates the origin of the distinction between time as form of inner intuition and space as form of outer intuition in the subject's identification with a signifier. To become a subject is to become a barred subject. This is to be understood in the specific sense that what a subject will be "for itself" as ego is cut off from what it is "in itself" simply because there is no "in itself" apart from the privileged signifier with which it is identified in the order of signifiers. Because this signifier exists as part of a network of signifiers, the subject's future sense of itself as a counting subject—i.e., the symbolic "meaning" of the ego—will eventually result from the schemata that link the network of signifiers to objects of intuition.

These schemata, I note in passing, are not analytic a posteriori judgments. As I have suggested, contra Kant, judgments only link signifiers; they do not link signifiers and objects of intuition. It is the schemata which refer judgments to possible objects of intuition. Put otherwise, on the side of the signifier, we have metonymic chains which can be classified as analytic a posteriori judgments. Insofar as a metaphoric substitution takes place, there appears what Lacan calls the "illusion" of crossing the bar that separates the order of signifiers (understanding) from the order of signifieds (sensibility) (Lacan 1977, 164). Hence a schema—a crossing of the bar—is something imaginary which takes place by way of metaphoric substitution. Or, more simply, schemata are metaphors.

Here we find a parallel between Lacan's account of the appearance of the signified at the level of subjectivity and my earlier speculation on the emergence of meaning in mathematics. In both cases, what seem to be at issue are "nonmeaningful" signifiers which can be brought into relation with each other. It is only insofar as these signifiers "make an appearance" in experience that they constitute the meaningful (i.e., what Lacan calls "the symbolic"). To say that a mathematical formula becomes meaningful only when applied to intuition could be rephrased by saying that it becomes meaningful through a process of metaphorization.

In the judgment "7 + 5 = 12," for example, the meaning of "7 + 5" will be what "7 + 5" represents for "12"—insofar as a metaphorical substitution is made whereby, say, "12" comes in to stand for "a certain number of wolves." This is not merely the Saussurean point that signification is a function of the structural relations among signifiers. In the absence of metaphorical schemata linking concepts to possible objects of experience, both "7 + 5" and "12" would remain nonmeaningful even after "7 + 5 = 12" had been accepted as "true" for the system of natural numbers. In other words, to operate at the level of the signifier alone would be to define mathematics in strictly metonymic terms; to introduce a metaphorical substitute is to link the system to that to which it purports to refer. Thus, only by way of (empirical) schemata do "7 + 5" and "12" indicate representational content for each other.

Lacan's statement that "the subject is what one signifier represents for another signifier" articulates the basic form of metaphorization. Specifically, the subject represents the locus of the meaningful only insofar as it is schematized by the signifiers that represent it. That is, just as "7 + 5 = 12" would become meaningful through the empirical activity of counting, so "I think therefore I am" would become meaningful through a schematization of the "I." There remains, however, a radical split between the schematizing subject and the schematized subject—what Lacan calls the split between the "subject of the enunciation" and the "subject of the enunciated statement" (Lacan 1978, 44).

The fact that subjectivity emerges as both the appearing of the inner/outer distinction and as the misidentification with a particular "outer" signifier illustrates Lacan's point that bodily image plays a role in the constituting of a subject's field of experience. This point finds its corollary in Kant, for whom the body appears as the original schematized object. There is thus a structural similarity in Kant between the role played by the body and by imagination, the faculty to which he attributes the work of schematization. Sarah Gibbons calls attention to this connection:

> The body remains distinct from nature while it is a part of nature; it *exhibits* the dual status of the subject and not simply its natural aspect. The body, then, stands in a similar relation to the self as does imagination: it mediates

> between the sensible and the intelligible, thereby making possible the act of judgement. (Gibbons 1994, 146)

Translating into Lacanian terminology, the body would be that privileged schematized object which functions as a kind of "quilting point," linking the field of signifiers to the field of signifieds.

Taking this suggestion one step further, Laura Hengehold argues in a fascinating article that for Kant not just bodily image but the body itself would have to play the role of a transcendental schema that "governs the separation of inner from outer" (Hengehold 1996, 2). Hengehold bases her argument on the "Refutation of Idealism" in which Kant claims that the appearance of objects of inner sense presupposes an awareness of something permanent in outer sense. Differing from commentators who have questioned whether the subject's body could be that permanent object in space which inner sense presupposes, Hengehold shows that the body would have to function not merely as an empirical object but as the transcendental schema that grounds the difference between inner and outer objects in the first place.

If we follow Hengehold in this regard, we could complicate some features of Freud's appeal to the primitive organism which learns to conceive a distinction between inner and outer sources of excitation. Freud treats the organism as if it already existed as a determinate body whose boundary would distinguish what is inside it from what is outside it. When the organism discovers that muscular movement can get rid of one set of excitations but not another, it discovers what already existed as an ontological fact—namely, that there is a real and more or less clear-cut distinction between itself and its environment. Freud's model, in other words, treats the organism's bodily boundaries as ontologically fixed; the only question he raises is the epistemological one of how the organism comes to recognize (or, perhaps, to fail to recognize) them. What Hengehold invites us to consider is whether what counts as a single body might already be the expression of something like a work of schematizing. Lacan's model of the imago as empirical schema for the subject's body suggests a way of working this suggestion out. Following Lacan, it would seem that we could not explain the inner/outer distinction simply by appealing to different muscular actions performed by an already demarcated bodily thing, for the very possibility of such activity to appear qua activity would already presuppose that something like an inner/outer distinction had been drawn.

Perhaps we can shed further light on this problem by referring to Nicolas Abraham and Maria Torok's way of developing the distinction between introjection and incorporation. Taking off from Freud's essay

"Mourning and Melancholia," Abraham and Torok argue that introjection is a process whereby a subject responds to loss by effecting some sort of topographical reconfiguration (Abraham and Torok 1994, 125). This process tends toward a redefining of the boundaries of the ego, specifically in the direction of their expansion. Incorporation, by contrast, takes place when the subject is for some reason unwilling to give up a previous topographical structure. Incorporation is the fantasy of having assimilated a loss without the subject's actually carrying out the work of decathexis which characterizes the normal process of introjection that takes place in mourning. Abraham and Torok seem to presume fantasy to be the work of the ego, and for this reason they criticize Melanie Klein for taking the fantasy of incorporation to be more primordial than the process of introjection. Introjection, they argue, plays a role in constituting the ego as an ego; following Klein, they hypothesize that the earliest occasion for introjection would be an infant's loss of its mother's breast.

As in the case of Freud's appeal to "the organism," Abraham and Torok seem to treat "the infant" as a clearly demarcated bodily thing teleologically oriented toward recognizing itself as such. The loss of an object (the mother's breast) is presumed to be the initial cause of its eventually attaining an idea of itself as subject. Once again, a potential problem with this model is that it presupposes what it is supposedly trying to explain. For how could the infant recognize a loss as a loss unless it had already attained some minimal distinction between self and Other, inner and outer? By presuming that fantasy is the work of the ego, Abraham and Torok seem to overlook the possibility that the distinction between inner and outer is a sort of primordial fantasy that cannot be easily contrasted with that of incorporation. On this point, we could refer not only to Lacan's insistence that to speak of the subject as split is not to presume that it has actually lost something which it once had, but also to his related argument that "reality" is always already framed by fantasy. The flip side of this, of course, is that fantasy itself refers back to that "primal cause" which cannot be reduced to fantasy—namely, an encounter with "the Real." Translating this double principle back into Freud's model of the primitive organism, we could characterize the posited excitations as "the Real," without additionally insisting on the metaphysical presumption that these excitations "belong to" or are "experienced by" an already demarcated bodily organism. In this sense, "excitations" would play a role strictly analogous to that played by the sensory manifold in Kant. Just as the sensory manifold is retroactively presumed to inaugurate experience only after fully schematized experience has appeared as the awareness of empirical objects by an empirical subject, so the supposed "primitive organism's" first excitations are retroactively presumed to inaugurate the appearance of an organism encountering objects in its environment.

In this context, we might put a different spin on Abraham and Torok's distinction between introjection and incorporation. Suppose we were to treat the primordial fantasy that makes a subject appear as a bodily thing to be the result of incorporation. An eventual offshoot of this unconscious fantasy would be the ego with the bodily idea to which it clings. Put otherwise, if the body consists of a network of ways of schematizing excitations (and here I deliberately avoid the misleading question as to who or what is doing the schematizing), then the ego would coincide with the meanings that these schemata come to have in their relation to one another. Any excitations that would call particular schemata into question could occasion either a process of introjection whereby the primordial fantasy might be reconfigured or a process of incorporation which would resist such reconfiguration. The fact that reconfiguration would appear as an "expansion" of the ego could be explained simply on the grounds that a larger set of excitations would have been coordinated with existing bodily schemata. The fact that a refusal or inability to reconfigure might lead to the formation of what Abraham and Torok call a crypt would be explained in terms of the conflict between new, spontaneously generated bodily schemata and existing bodily schemata.

In the "Metapsychological Supplement to the Theory of Dreams" (*SE* XIV), Freud raises the question of why it is that unconscious drives do not generally tend (except in the rare instance of somnambulism) to manifest themselves through motor discharge during sleep. Perhaps the model developed here suggests a way of answering this question. Suppose, modifying Hengehold's suggestion slightly, we treat the body as a network of *empirical* schemata which express (possibly conflicting) ways of distinguishing the inner from the outer. To say that the subject "has a body" would be to say that its experience has become structured by a particular configuration of instinctual demands which have reached the level of consciousness. Repression could then be correlated with the ego's rejection of those drives which would either alter its body over time or force it to reconfigure its bodily image; the "strength" of repression would be a function of the ego's introjective fluidity. Repressed drives would tend toward alternative spatiotemporal configurations corresponding to unschematized possible bodily images. When the subject is asleep, the ego's "normal" bodily image would be relaxed, allowing these repressed drives to manifest themselves. Perhaps a main function of dreaming would be to exhibit a certain spatiotemporal experimentation resulting from the release of repressed drives and the consequent imaginative construction of possible bodily images. The fact that the inner/outer distinction would be in disarray would account for the fact that dreams rarely exhibit clearly demarcated boundaries between subject and object. If we further assume, with Lacan and others, that motor activity presupposes the fixing of a bodily image, it will naturally follow that dreams rarely give form to stable enough schemata to allow for motor activity to take place. The dreamer would be like an infant who does not yet have a fixed form; the dream itself would be like an experimentation with a variety of possible "imagos." In short, such dreams would mark a return to the mirror stage, where it is not yet clear what will count as a bodily image. Of course, there might also be dreams in which what was at issue was not regression to the mirror stage but regression to the echo stage. There it would not be the body qua object of outer intuition but the body qua object of inner intuition whose uncertain status would be at stake.

Part of the task of psychoanalysis would be to treat hysterical bodily symptoms and obsessional modes of bodily comportment as evidence of either introjective fluidity or incorporative fixity, and in this way to analyze a subject's "forms of intuition." As is well known, Kant conducted himself in a manner typical of obsessional neurotics: he trained his body to obey rigid temporal laws—e.g., rules about when to walk, where to walk, how to move his feet, etc. Perhaps the best way of characterizing such an aesthetic would be to say that it is determined by a *subsumption of the spatial under temporal laws*—which, of course, is precisely how Kant treats the schemata of the understanding in general. In this way, he tries to deny the split between the subject of inner sense (subject of the enunciation) and the subject of outer sense (subject of the enunciated statement). That is, Kant does not merely assume the position of the subject of the enunciation at the cost of relegating his body to the position of the subject of the enunciated; he attempts to deny the spatiality of the subject altogether. This would explain why Kant sometimes seems to treat the body as an object of outer intuition alone; as Quassim Cassam has pointed out, Kant does not appear to consider inner sense to be in any way the intuition of bodily states (Cassam 1993, 122–24).

Kant's inability to arrive at a satisfactory account of the relationship between inner sense and outer sense is evidenced in his various attempts to make sense of the phenomenon of incongruent counterparts—a phenomenon which bears an obvious resemblance to the inversion of mirror images described by Lacan. In his attempt to demonstrate the synthetic a priori character of geometrical judgments, Kant argues that it would be impossible to distinguish a right-hand glove from a left-hand glove merely by means of concepts. In an early precritical essay, he took the significance of this phenomenon to lie with the fact that the gloves can be known to be incongruous counterparts only if space exists as an absolute frame of reference (Kant 1992, 371). By the time of the *Prolegomena,* his argument is that only an appeal to intuition could determine which was the right-hand glove and which the left-hand glove (Kant 1977, 29–30). But this capacity itself requires that the subject represent itself as existing in space, for only with respect to its body can it distinguish between "right-hand" and "left-hand." Were the body identified merely through outer sense, however, it would remain just as nonoriented as the gloves. Presumably, it can only be through the subject's identification of itself with its body that it can ground the orientation of objects in general, but this is precisely what the subject of inner sense cannot do. For this reason, Luce Irigaray—who reads Kant as part of a long tradition that associates masculinity with time and femininity with space—highlights Kant's inability to solve the problem (Irigaray 1985, 203–13).

Obviously, similar questions concerning proprioception and kinaesthesis would have to be raised here as well, particularly as such phenomena could be said to reveal structures which cannot be reduced to objects of either inner or outer sense. The fact that Kant himself was not willing to consider inner sense as bodily awareness suggests that he simply did not take these phenomena to pose a problem for the division of his transcendental aesthetic.

Once again, we find here a difference between Kant and Hume. That the subject has no impression with which it can "properly" identify indicates for Hume that the distinction between inner and outer experience is ultimately problematic. What I think of as my body is simply a result of habit (incorporation), as is revealed in the experience of "phantom" limbs; and there is nothing whatsoever that could correspond to my idea of myself qua subject of thought. Hence, for Hume the ideas of both space and time are not predicated on a subject/object dichotomy as they are for Kant; they are the ideas that result from a gathering of impressions which gathering cannot be identified with the activity of a subject. In short, apperception is not something carried out by an agent; or, to put the point in Heideggerian language, apperception is perhaps to be thought of as the "worlding of the world" which gives rise to those structures of finitude that can always be accompanied by an "I think."

This is a point to which I will return in the next chapter. For here, it is important to emphasize that for Kant schemata are ways of synthesizing time. At issue is not simply the body as spatial border between inner and outer but the body as a structure for deciding which future excitations will be considered as belonging to the subject and which as not belonging to it. This is why, as Žižek points out, it is so easy to read Kant as an obsessional neurotic (Žižek 1993, 70). What is curious about the Kantian model is that it exteriorizes the idea of the body from the idea of the subject by dictating that *all* excitations should be external (the elimination of pathological content from the will); precisely here we see not the obsessional but the perverse side of Kant. The fact that Kant could not avoid recognizing some excitations as internal led, ultimately, to a phobic relation to the flow of excitations—a situation I discuss in somewhat different terms in my book *Discipline and Critique* (Cutrofello 1994, 48–63).

Of course, a "normal" subject might be expected to be both hysterical and obsessional to different degrees; as such, we would find both bodily symptoms and a mode of temporal comportment. In this sense, moreover, every living body will be more or less normal, for even the hysteric and the obsessional will exhibit both temporal and spatial symptoms; the hysteric will "geometrize" time just as the obsessional will temporalize space. Thus, for example, the Rat Man exhibits the "curvature" of his space through the convoluted itinerary he follows with an eye toward fulfilling his self-imposed duty to return the borrowed money to the lieutenant (*SE* X, 168ff.). Conversely, in anxiety hysteria the subject's anxious relationship to time might be said to result precisely from the impossibility of foreclosing the temporal altogether.

In using the language of spatial and temporal "curvature," I do not mean to suggest that we can map the neuroses against a "normal" aesthetic for which space and time would not be curved. Kant's own transcendental aesthetic is intended to represent the way in which "normal" subjects represent the world, but it is clear that every construct of space and time would represent a particular "curvature." We can no more indicate a normal way of intuiting space and time than we could a normal way of walking. Kant's own mechanized daily stroll happens to reveal an especially obsessional model, but it is not as if we can compare it to "Euclidean walking."

If I walk the way I do because I believe that my feet are colonized by millions of tiny bugs with poisonous venom, then the manner in which I walk cannot be explained solely in terms of the spatiotemporal logic of the neuroses. Here I would have introduced dynamical connections into the basis for my judgment, suggesting that my symptoms represent something on the order of a psychosis rather than a neurosis. Once again, I am trying to narrow the scope of the term *neurosis* to cover purely aesthetic constructs of time and space (though I will complicate this account somewhat in chapters 3 and 4).

The ability to question the grounds of a condition which functions as if it were a transcendental limit requires that we not allow this limit to constrict our thought-experiments. One way of avoiding this problem is to treat the limit itself as the effect of a cause that is not subject to it. This is the strategy at work in Plato's cave analogy. By treating the objects of sensibility as shadows, Plato was able to imagine the possibility of nonsensible objects. (A somewhat similar idea led Marcel Duchamp to think of three-dimensional objects as the cast shadows of four-dimensional objects.) For Freud and Lacan, it is the idea that the distinction between inner and outer intuition might be an effect of projection and identification that enables them to treat space and time as grounded in something that might elude the limits of Euclidean representation. It is for this reason, I take it, that topological objects (in the mathematical sense) play such a prominent role in Lacan's metapsychological speculations—he refers at one point to "life's touching strivings after topological configurations" (Lacan 1978, 147)—and why the task of providing a transcendental aesthetic gives way to the task of providing a typology of neuroses.

# 3

# Logics of Perversion

> It must be possible for the "I think" to accompany all my representations.
> —Kant 1965, B131

> Where id was, there ego shall be.
> —Freud *SE* XXII, 80

If the neuroses are aesthetic, then the perversions are conceptual—for in perversion, what remains consigned to the level of sensibility appears at the level of judging consciousness—i.e., at the level of understanding. Part of what would distinguish perverse subjects from neurotics, then, would be the fact that perverse subjects *theorize* their symptoms—witness the writings of Sade.

Freud suggests that perversion can be characterized as a kind of defense against both neuroses and psychoses (*SE* XIX, 152–53), a suggestion he would later hint at more fully in his unfinished essay on the splitting of the ego (*SE* XXIII). If neuroses result from the repression of an instinctual urge in favor of the demands of reality, and if psychoses result from the rejection of reality in favor of the demands of the id (*SE* XIX, 149)—a suggestion Freud later complicates but does not abandon—then perversions could be thought of as compromises between the two. Of course, Freud also defines normality as a compromise between neurosis and psychosis (*SE* XIX, 185)—a coincidence which only serves to underscore the difficulty, if not impossibility, of drawing any sharp distinction between normal and perverse subjects (*SE* VII, 50).

In his essay "Kant with Sade," Lacan argues that what appear in Kant to be normal principles of morality are in fact virtually indistinguishable from Sadean principles of perversion. Lacan traces the supposed synthetic a priori character of the categorical imperative back to an experience of loss which Kant never explicitly acknowledges—a loss which, because of its tie to the empirical, would undermine the pretensions to a "pure" deduction of not only the categorical imperative but of the categories of the understanding as well (Lacan 1989, 61–63).

Obviously, Kant's argument depends upon his claim to have discovered synthetic a priori judgments. Were he to acknowledge that these same judgments might be treated as analytic a posteriori, he would have to confront Lacan's call for "a new Critique of Reason hinging upon the impure" (Lacan 1989, 63). In order to forestall such a possibility, Kant insists not only on the synthetic a priori character of those judgments which are symptomatic of structures of experience, but also on the necessity to purge transcendental philosophy of all reference to psychology—especially what he calls "empirical" psychology. Toward this end, he establishes the parameters of a purely transcendental *logic.*

Just as Kant claims that synthetic a priori judgments in mathematics show we can distinguish pure from empirical intuitions, so he argues that synthetic a priori judgments in science show we can distinguish between "pure and empirical thought of objects":

> Since, as the Transcendental Aesthetic has shown, there are pure as well as empirical intuitions, a distinction might likewise be drawn between pure and empirical thought of objects. In that case we should have a logic in which we do not abstract from the entire content of knowledge. (A55/B79–80)

However, whereas mathematics already exists as a body of synthetic a priori knowledge, it is only with the *Critique of Pure Reason* that a comparable body of synthetic a priori knowledge in science first appears. Kant calls this body of knowledge "transcendental logic" in contrast to the "general logic" developed by Aristotle. Aristotelian logic concerns itself with the study of the rules of thought, but it focuses exclusively on the mere form of thought in general, not on that content which can be thought of objects independently of experience. Where "general logic" abstracts from all specific contents of particular thoughts, transcendental logic has at its disposal whatever a priori forms thoughts can take in reference to the pure forms of intuition.

A complete exposition of transcendental logic comprises both the systematic explication of the rules of pure thought, and the attempt to elucidate "the origin of the modes in which we know objects" (A55–56/B80). The question of origin here concerns not only the question of whether a particular concept is pure or empirical, but also the task of identifying the specific faculty from which a particular mode of cognition arises. The latter will help to determine the limits of the proper employment which such an origin entails. The question concerning origins can go no further than this; Kant does not believe that transcendental logic can accomplish anything by speculating on how or why the faculties come to be structured as they are. In short, Kant thinks he can describe the topography of the psychic apparatus but not its genesis.

Both transcendental logic and general logic share a common trait: they are both concerned with the pure as opposed to the empirical nature of thought. Kant accordingly draws a sharp distinction between "pure" and "applied" logic. In the case of general logic he writes:

> Pure general logic has to do . . . only with principles *a priori,* and is a *canon of understanding* and reason, but only in respect of what is formal in their employment, be the content what it may, empirical or transcendental. General logic is called applied, when it is directed to the rules of the employment of understanding under the subjective empirical conditions dealt with by psychology. (A53/B77)

By strictly separating empirical psychology (applied logic) from pure general logic, Kant seeks to show why transcendental logic, though it goes beyond the bounds of general logic, is not itself a form of psychology. At several points of his subsequent exposition, he underscores this point by noting when a particular topic—for example, the reproductive (as opposed to the productive) synthesis of the imagination—"falls within the domain, not of transcendental philosophy, but of psychology" (B152). Elsewhere he notes that, while the concept of freedom "does indeed concern psychology" its "treatment and solution belong exclusively to transcendental philosophy" (A535/B503).

Kant's attempt to maintain a clear-cut distinction between transcendental philosophy and empirical psychology runs into difficulties, however. Aside from the problem of there being psychologistic overtones in the doctrine of the faculties, several key arguments—notably, that of the "subjective" deduction—seem to presuppose introspective descriptions of empirical thought. This fact has led some of Kant's critics to argue that transcendental philosophy is itself guilty of a certain form of psychologism.

Seeking to defend Kant against this charge, Patricia Kitcher has emphasized the differences between a merely empirical psychology and a genuinely transcendental psychology. Kitcher concedes that even the latter requires some minimal reference to evidence of introspection, but she maintains that Kant's appeal to facts about human cognitive capacities does not "rest on a fallacy of confusing the normative with the factual." Transcendental arguments are only "weakly psychologistic" in that they treat empirical facts about human cognitive abilities as "important to philosophical or normative claims, even though they cannot establish such claims" (Kitcher 1990, 9). Transcendental arguments, unlike hypothetical epistemic analyses, purport to demonstrate not only information about how humans happen to think but also the fact that the world necessarily conforms to the requirements of human cognition. According to Kant, "the conditions of the *possibility of experience* in general are likewise conditions for the *possibility of the objects of experience*" (A158/B197). Merely hypothetical epistemic analyses can show only what would have to obtain in the world for human knowledge to be possible, and Kant, of course, is not satisfied with such a skeptical result. But if, Kitcher argues, we can make an empirical appeal to the acquisition of human knowledge, then transcendental philosophy might be able to overcome this dificulty (Kitcher 1990, 19–20).

An obvious problem, of course, is that the Humean question can always arise as to whether humans do actually possess empirical knowledge of the world. Furthermore, even the most minimal appeal to empirical facts about human cognition would seem to undermine Kant's insistence on the pure character of transcendental logic. Kitcher is willing to give up the stringency of this demand, arguing that we can still distinguish transcendental psychology from both introspective and behavioral models by the specificity of its object—the knowing subject. "Transcendental psychology is the psychology of the thinking, or better, knowing, self" (Kitcher 1990, 22). The knowing self is the subject of apperception which, on Kant's account, is neither a mere object of intuition nor a noumenal object which we could know through intellectual intuition. Kitcher takes issue with Kant's treatment of the subject of apperception, however, describing it as "a third self" that differs from both the phenomenal and noumenal subjects (Kitcher 1990, 21). Once we give up extraneous commitments to the phenomena/noumena distinction, she suggests, there is no good reason to treat the thinking subject as distinct from the phenomenal subject:

> Kant resists placing the thinking self in the phenomenal realm. . . . Given his own doctrine of noumena, and an exhaustive dichotomy, however, the thinking self must be phenomenal. Hence, transcendental psychology must be empirical, in this sense, even though it is very different from what he regarded as "empirical psychology." (Kitcher 1990, 22)

Kitcher goes on to develop a rich account of this weakly empirical transcendental psychology, though at the expense of rejecting Kant's arguments about why the unity of apperception cannot be classified as either phenomenal or noumenal. She presumes that Kant's chief reason for treating the unity of apperception as distinct from the phenomenal subject was to safeguard his solution to the Third Antinomy:

> Given the impossibility of noumenal knowledge, the doctrine of apperception must present a phenomenal, if highly abstract, aspect of the self. If Kant is right that anything of which we can have knowledge must be governed by causal laws, then synthetic connection will be lawful. . . . The I that thinks will be phenomenal and causally determined. This is, however, too close to us. It is the I with which we identify. What possible comfort—or even interest—could we have in knowing that some noumenal self is free and potentially immortal, when the self with which we identify, the thinker, is phenomenal? I believe that Kant refuses to acknowledge the phenomenal character of the doctrine of apperception to avoid this devastating implication. I see no other coherent alternative, however. (Kitcher 1990, 139–40)

Kitcher's argument supposes that Kant is trying to fit a three-self model into a two-world framework. However, the transcendental subject need not be interpreted as a "third subject"; instead we might think of it as a function of the something-I-know-not-what which the thinking subject takes itself to be. In other words, for Kant the transcendental subject *is* the noumenal subject insofar as it knows nothing about itself other than the fact that it unifies appearances of itself as empirical subject. Far from there being three subjects here, on my reading there are not even two. For in the end Kant thinks that there is only one subject—the noumenal subject—which, through the transcendental function that tells it nothing about what it is, presents it with an empirical appearance of itself. Thus, the thinking subject is cut off from itself in such a way as to make the unity of apperception impossible to classify either as noumenal or as phenomenal. As Žižek puts it:

> The status of Kant's I of transcendental apperception is that of a *necessary* and simultaneously *impossible* logical construction ("impossible" in the precise sense that its notion can never be filled out with intuited experiential reality), in short: of the Lacanian *real.* (Žižek 1993, 14)

However, whereas the Lacanian "Real" can never be filled, the Kantian subject identifies precisely with itself qua Real—i.e., qua noumenal. Or, to put the matter otherwise, the Kantian subject of apperception realizes, qua split subject, that its imago (phenomenal appearance) is a lure, but it maintains a belief in itself as ultimately being a full subject.

In a footnote to the second edition version of the Paralogisms, Kant writes:

> The "I think" expresses an indeterminate empirical intuition, i.e. perception. . . . But the "I think" precedes the experience which is

> required to determine the object of perception through the category in respect of time. . . . An indeterminate perception here signifies only something real that is given [*etwas Reales das gegeben worden*], given indeed to thought in general, and so not as appearance, nor as thing in itself (*noumenon*), but as something which actually exists [*etwas, was in der Tat existiert*], and which in the proposition, "I think," is denoted as such. (B422–423n.)

Kant's remarks on the unity of apperception seem, at first, to throw a monkey-wrench into the view that the phenomena/noumena dichotomy exhausts all possible ways of conceiving of things that exist. Conversely, though, it sheds light on how we should make use of this dichotomy. According to Kant, the idea of the noumenon arises out of reflection on the concept of the transcendental object (A249/B306). Likewise, from the concept of the transcendental subject, reflection arrives at the concept of itself as noumenon. Just as we can think the transcendental object either phenomenally or noumenally, so we can think the transcendental subject in either of these ways. But the fact remains that both the concept of the transcendental object and the concept of the transcendental subject (i.e., the "I think") mark *limits* which for Kant divide the phenomenal from the noumenal. Thus, the unity of apperception is simply the limit—or the split—within the noumenal subject (whatever it is) that makes it radically other than what it appears to itself to be. Of course, the entire difference between Kant and Lacan could be articulated by noting that whereas Kant insists that the subject "really" is this lost noumenal (or "full") subject, Lacan will identify the subject precisely with the split of apperception itself (see Žižek 1993).

Kitcher's question concerns what would seem to be the Kantian dilemma of how to ontologize the split subject of apperception, given that we seem to have to choose between calling it phenomenal or noumenal. I take it, however, that Kant implicitly avoids this either/or choice by way of a tacit invocation of the logical function of the infinite judgment. Instead of merely claiming that the unity of apperception is not phenomenal (which would be a negative judgment), Kant in effect suggests that the subject recognizes itself as *nonphenomenal.* By reflecting on the fact that the only judgments that refer to it are infinite judgments, the subject can deny the phenomenal character of its "I think" without having to classify itself as noumenal. Although he does not make this point explicitly, Kant does refer to the concept of the soul when he seeks to illustrate the function of the infinite judgment:

> Now by the proposition, "The soul is non-mortal," I have, so far as the logical form is concerned, really made an affirmation. I locate the soul in

> the unlimited sphere of non-mortal beings. . . . The infinite sphere of all that is possible is thereby only so far limited that the mortal is excluded from it. . . . But, even allowing for such exclusion, this extension still remains infinite, and several more parts of it may be taken away *without the concept of the soul being thereby in the least increased, or determined in an affirmative manner.* (A72–73/B97–98; my italics)

That Kant takes the "I think" to be determined only by way of infinite judgments would also seem to be supported by the famous passage from the Paralogisms chapter:

> We can assign no other basis for this teaching than the simple, and in itself completely empty, representation "I"; and we cannot even say that this is a concept, but only that it is a bare consciousness which accompanies all concepts. Through this I or he or it (the thing) which thinks, nothing further is represented than a transcendental subject of the thoughts = X. (A345–46/B403–4)

The subject of apperception is arrived at by a process of, so to speak, "infinitely negating" every particular phenomenal content of experience: I am non-this, non-that, etc. Based on how the subject formulates the concept of itself as thinking subject, in other words, the "I" of apperception cannot be, as Kitcher would have it, something phenomenal. On the contrary, it is revealed in every phenomenal experience as "not being that either, whatever else it is."

Of course, by continuing to take the problems posed by the Paralogisms seriously, Kant in effect submits the subject to the telos of affirmative judgments, even if the subject itself cannot determine their content. What is this move, in fact, but the submission of the subject to the unfathomable law of the categorical imperative? In contrast to Kant, Lacan might be said to leave the question concerning the subject "in itself" at the level of the infinite judgment. Put otherwise, there is no subject for Lacan outside the slippery slope of metonymy—until, of course, the subject finds itself metaphorically schematized in a bodily imago (which remains a lure).

If we do not follow Kitcher in collapsing the distinction between the subject qua limit on self-knowledge and the subject as it appears to itself, but accept her argument that something like transcendental psychology might require a weak rather than a strong appeal to empirical introspection, we can easily see where the specificity of a metapsychological inquiry would arise. At his most epistemically rigorous moments, Freud steers a middle course between psychologism and transcendentalism. The problematic of apperception, for Freud, would lie with interrogating the limit that separates the subject from itself qua ego. Such interrogations are weakly psychologistic in that they presuppose some acquaintance with the acts whereby the subject is represented by the ego. But they are not strongly psychologistic, for they do not reduce the question of the limit of apperception (the unconscious) to either an introspective or a behaviorist investigation. Construed in this way, metapsychology would be reducible neither to "empirical" nor to "rational" psychology in Kant's sense of these terms.

The chief problem with rational psychology, for Kant, is that it purports to know the subject as a thing in itself. Discussing the paralogisms, he notes the impossibility of gaining insight into the nature of the soul from a supposedly pure rational psychology, arguing that such attempts invariably depend on illicit empirical psychological observations (A347/B405). Interestingly, he invokes in this context the case of excitations of pleasure (*Lust*) and displeasure (*Unlust*): "The least object of perception (for example, even pleasure or displeasure), if added to the universal representation of self-consciousness, would at once transform rational psychology into empirical psychology" (A343/B401).

In the case of empirical psychology, things are not so straightforward, for here the problem is not just the converse fact that empirical psychology is limited to providing scientific knowledge of the phenomenal subject. Were empirical psychology capable of giving us such knowledge it would amount to what Kant calls "a kind of *physiology* of inner sense" (A347/B405), but in fact it cannot even provide this much. The reason for this has to do with a dissymmetry between the mathematics of time and the mathematics of space. According to Kant, all scientific knowledge depends upon mathematical knowledge, a point he makes in the *Metaphysical Foundations of Natural Science*: "Since in every doctrine of nature only so much science proper is to be found as there is a priori cognition in it, a doctrine of nature will contain only so much science proper as there is applied mathematics in it" (Kant 1985, 7). On this basis, Kant considers mechanics to be more rigorously scientific than chemistry, arguing that the latter seems to be more of "a systematic art or experimental doctrine" than "science proper" (Kant 1985, 7). But the least scientific of all investigations into nature is empirical psychology. This is because there is no applied mathematics in this field. Whereas observations of objects in space allow for an application of mathematical principles to the study of motion, observation of the subject's experiences over time might allow at most for the plotting of a straight line:

> Mathematics is inapplicable to the phenomena of the internal sense and their laws, unless one might want to take into consideration merely the

> law of continuity in the flow of this sense's internal changes. But the extension of cognition so attained would bear much the same relation to the extension of cognition which mathematics provides for the doctrine of body, as the doctrine of the properties of the straight line bears to the whole of geometry. The reason for the limitation on this extension of cognition lies in the fact that the pure internal intuition in which the soul's phenomena are to be constructed is time, which has only one dimension. (Kant 1985, 8)

Were empirical psychology to attempt to ground itself as a natural science it could do nothing other than plot a line as the (spatial) representation of a possible succession of objects of inner sense. This line would tell us nothing about how or why objects of intuition succeed each other in the order in which they do; it would indicate the form of a merely descriptive listing of the succession of inner events—i.e., "and then . . . , and then . . . ," etc.

Here it is interesting to consider whether developments in mathematics since Kant's day would force him to complicate this picture. Topology—which, interestingly, had already found expression in Kant's day in Euler's solution to the problem of the "Königsberg Bridges"—is in many ways an offshoot of geometry, but one whose development required that appeals to intuition be given up. According to Stephen Barr, topology can be thought of as "the study of continuity: beginning with the continuity of space, or shapes, it generalizes, and then by analogy leads into other kinds of continuity" (Barr 1989, 2). More precisely, "a topologist is interested in those properties of a thing that, while they are in a sense geometrical, are the most permanent—the ones that will survive distortion and stretching" (Barr 1989, 2–3).

For Kant, it will be remembered, time is the form by which the continuity of the subject's experience is given. Yet Kant takes arithmetic, not topology, to provide a mathematical model of time. Even if we were to grant that the line is the basic form of time, topology shows that lines are far richer in their mathematical possibilities than Kant suggests: "In topology, . . . the straight line doesn't have to remain straight: but it retains the quality of being continuously connected along itself, and with its ends disconnected—or not, as the case may be" (Barr 1989, 3–4).

What if, without ceasing to be a "line," time could undergo topological transformation? Would this provide a mathematical basis for something like empirical psychology? In the previous chapter, I argued that the neuroses might be thought of in terms of curvatures of time and space. Clearly, it is but a short step to reading Lacan's mathematized version of Freudian "topology" as attempting to account for the topological transformations that find expression in the neuroses. In this context, it is amusing to read the following in Barr: "Topology started as a kind of geometry, but it has reached into many other mathematical fields. One might almost say it is a state of mind—and is its own goal" (Barr 1989, 2).

Here, the question might arise as to whether Lacan's references to topological objects constitute an attempt to ground a pure as opposed to an empirical metapsychology. Certainly it might seem possible to inscribe, within Kantianism, a transcendental deduction of the possibility of metapsychology. But in order to carry through such a project, it would be necessary to question the limits of the faculties as they are dogmatically described by transcendental philosophy. As the study of topological transformations requires that we give up the pretension to synthetic a priori knowledge, the task which Kitcher assigns to transcendental psychology would give way to psychoanalysis. More so than transcendental psychology, psychoanalysis requires that we call into question the distinction between pure transcendental inquiry and empirical inquiry. In this sense, then, any "deduction" of metapsychology might be better read as a deconstruction of the claims of transcendental philosophy rather than as a further development of them.

That Kant repeatedly verges on blurring the distinction between the pure and the empirical is a point that Kitcher brings out well. Kant seems willing to concede that practical philosophy must be weakly empirical in Kitcher's sense; thus, in the first edition of the *Critique,* he suggests that the "fundamental concepts of morality" lie outside transcendental philosophy, because they presuppose the empirical concepts of pain, pleasure, desire, etc. (A15). In the introduction, he clarifies this point by indicating the difference between the way in which morality appeals to the empirical and the way in which other branches of knowledge do. The concepts of morality:

> do not lay at the foundation of their precepts the concepts of pleasure and pain [*Lust und Unlust*], of the desires and inclinations, etc., . . . yet in the construction of a system of pure morality these empirical concepts must necessarily be brought into the concept of duty. (A15/B28–29)

Thus, as Lacan reminds us, Kant claims to be able to deduce from the moral law the necessity of the subject's experiencing its duty as painful (Lacan 1992, 80). Nonetheless, Kant insists that there is a difference between a moral system from which we might deduce certain pathological implications and a moral psychology which would attempt to construct a moral theory by appeal to the pathological.

In the *Groundwork*, Kant attacks moral psychology of the Wolffian variety, calling it at best a mere "propadeutic" that will "differ from a metaphysics of morals in the same way that general logic . . . differs from transcendental philosophy" (Kant 1981, 390). This suggests that what Kant calls applied logic—"a cathartic of the common understanding" (A53/B78) which "treats of attention, its impediments and consequences, of the source of error, of the state of doubt, hesitation, and conviction, etc." (A54/B79)—might similarly serve as a propadeutic to transcendental philosophy, but never as a substitute for it. Kant warns his reader to be on guard:

> But we must be careful, in turning our attention to an object which is foreign to transcendental philosophy, that we do not indulge in digressions to the detriment of the unity of the system, nor on the other hand, by saying too little on this new topic, fail in producing conviction through lack of clearness. I hope to avoid both dangers, by keeping as close as possible to the transcendental [*daß ich mich so nahe als mögliche am Transzendentalen halte*], and by leaving entirely aside any psychological, that is, empirical, factors that may perchance accompany it. (A801/B829)

At issue, Kant suggests, is merely an expository problem of how to keep two distinct levels of analysis separate. Yet the very idea of "keeping as close as possible to the transcendental" should make us wonder if it is only a question of degree whether an argument is "more psychological" or "more transcendental."

This potential ambiguity becomes most obvious and of most crucial importance at the very heart of the *Critique*—in Kant's presentation of the Deductions. Critical dissatisfaction with the argument of the Metaphysical Deduction is of course widespread; even Klaus Reich, who defends its unity and rigor, relies on texts outside the Deduction proper to support his reading. In presenting the Table of Judgments, Kant famously offers little in the way of justificatory argumentation, seeming to take for granted, with slight modifications, the basic classificatory scheme of traditional logic (A70–71/B95–96). As Reich shows, however, there is a deeper unity that motivates Kant's exposition.

Kant claims to start with the Table of Judgments, from this to deduce the Table of Categories, and from there to proceed via the Transcendental Deduction to an account of the Principles of the Understanding. But it is only at the level of the principles that we find those judgments which he identifies as synthetic a priori. No wonder, then, that the Transcendental Analytic can be read as proceeding backwards. If the aim of the *Critique* is to account for the possibility of synthetic a priori judgments, then strictly speaking we would expect Kant to start with the principles and work from there to the two tables. The problem, of course, is that those of Kant's readers coming from Hume will not immediately accept that the principles are a priori, for these concern "matters of fact"—though Humeans could be expected to accept the a priori character of mathematical judgments, as these seem to concern "relations of ideas."

Without the grounding provided by the deductions, Kant cannot establish the a priori character of the principles; yet without the principles, he cannot justify his invocation of the tables. Perhaps the supplement of the synthetic presentation of the *Critique* by the analytic presentation of the *Prolegomena* is not merely a rhetorical convenience, as Kant would have it, but a requirement of the justificatory demands of transcendental philosophy (Kant 1977, 8). Going back and forth between judgments and their supposed transcendental foundations would suggest not a vicious circle but a hermeneutic circle; the question is whether the requirement of such a circle entails an irreducible appeal to psychological introspection.

Here we can see why Kitcher's reading of Kant is so compelling, for it suggests a way of "saving" the claims of a weakly empiricist transcendental psychology. On the other hand, any admission of the empirical (weak or strong) into transcendental inquiry should make us wonder if the judgments which Kant identifies as synthetic a priori are truly a priori. It is here that the metapsychological alternative suggests itself, and it is worth recalling that metapsychology in no way presupposes the validity of introspective appeals. Rather than assume the correctness of descriptions of human cognitive capacities, metapsychology begins only with the fact of these descriptions themselves. Where a Kantian might ultimately have no better recourse than to insist that a certain judgment is synthetic a priori because our introspective evidence is what it is, the psychoanalyst would seek only to question why a judgment might appear to make reference to an a priori structure of experience. Accordingly, the question that needs to be considered with respect to the Kantian Analytic is, as expected: what follows if we treat the principles of understanding which Kant calls synthetic a priori as analytic a posteriori?

The purported a priori character of the principles of the understanding depends not only on the claim that the categories (and their corresponding forms of judgment) are a priori, but also on the claim that these categories are necessarily applicable to all possible objects of experience. The whole point of the Transcendental Deduction is to show not only that we *do* use the categories in a certain way but that we are *entitled* to do so. To confirm, contra Hume, that objective knowledge about the world is possible, it is not enough to establish the fact that we structure experience in a particular way. Nor would it suffice to show that we do so in accordance with concepts that are a priori. We would also need to establish that the objects of our experience necessarily conform to these a priori concepts with which we spontaneously structure experience.

Since the aim of a metapsychological antithetic to Kant's *Critique* is to interrogate the forms of experience which Kant identifies, we can accept his descriptive claims simply as clinical evidence—i.e., as an analysand's statements about how he takes human experience to be structured. Just as the psychoanalyst takes a dream-report at face value without worrying about whether it accurately reflects the dream "itself," so we can treat Kant's account of the limits of experience as something like his "limits-of-experience-report." That this in no way guarantees that Kant is accurately describing the limits of his experience is irrelevant.

According to Kant, the categories are applied to objects of experience by a spontaneity of the understanding. To plumb the depths of this spontaneity, he says, is impossible. We can no more hope to fathom why we think in terms of the specific categories with which we do think than we could determine why we intuit the world as being in space and time (B145–146). To be sure, there is room for empirical psychology and anthropology to consider the evolution of human cognitive faculties. But such an enterprise can observe only processes of maturation, not the origin of the faculties themselves. Transcendental philosophy explicitly precludes the very possibility of explaining human cognition in terms of what Kant calls, usually when referring to Locke, a "*physiology* of the human understanding" (Aix). Any physical reductionism, for example, would be guilty of an amphiboly of reflection. By ruling out the very intelligibility of speculation as to where we get the categories from, Kant not only wards off the bad transcendent metaphysics which he maintains would characterize such speculation, he also lends rhetorical support to his claim that he has correctly identified the only possible set of categories in terms of which human thought must be structured.

Freud, I have noted, tries to account for the origin of the distinction between inner and outer experience in terms of an organism's perception of a difference between those painful stimuli which it can avoid by motor activity (judged to be external to the organism) and those which it cannot avoid (judged to be internal). In "Instincts and Their Vicissitudes," Freud presents this hypothesis in a deliberately speculative fashion: "Let us imagine ourselves in the position of an almost entirely helpless organism, as yet unoriented in the world. . . ." On Freud's account, those stimuli which the organism takes to be internal can be thought of as having an instinctual basis. We imagine an instinct, or drive, to be a spontaneous impulse within the organism which demands that the organism seek out an object to satisfy it. It is not the sight of food which causes me to be hungry but hunger which makes me look for food. Of course, the sight of food can occasion in me a manifestation of my hunger or cause me to act as I do when I am in fact hungry: to this extent, the presentation of an object to my senses can be an occasion for a spontaneous response whereby I come to think of that object as something that I can eat.

Perhaps we can apply this model for thinking about the spontaneity of the understanding as Kant describes it. An object of sensibility becomes an occasion for a spontaneous response whereby the faculty of understanding subsumes the object under a set of categories. Suppose we were to imagine that there were a "cognitive drive"—perhaps related to what Freud calls scopophilia (*SE* VII, 156–57)—at work determining the spontaneity that Kant identifies.

One possible objection to thinking of Kant's spontaneity of understanding in terms of a cognitive drive would be that the "stimulus" that calls forth this spontaneity would seem to be not internal but external. After all, it is the appearance of an object of intuition that occasions the use we make of the categories in the first place. To this extent, there might seem to be a disanalogy with the food/hunger example cited above. But here we should recall the opening words of the second edition of the *Critique*: "There can be no doubt that all our knowledge begins [*anfange*] with experience. . . . But though all our knowledge begins [*anhebt*] with experience, it does not follow that it all arises [*entspringt*] out of experience" (B1). One way of translating this into a Freudian vocabulary would be to say that, although all drives presuppose objects toward which they are directed, it does not follow that everything in the drives arises out of these objects. If the spontaneity of the understanding were to be construed as a cathexis directed toward an object of intuition, it would be quite plausible to imagine that the stimulus to judge would be "originary" in some sense. The object of intuition would be construed as the cause of judgment only as a result of projection (or, in Kantian terminology, as a result of an amphibolous misattribution of something to the receptive faculty of sensibility that belongs to the faculty of understanding).

In the primitive apparatus of the organism which Freud posits, what will later count as external stimuli initially occasion motor responses, not cognitive responses, in the organism. Concepts make their appearance only at a higher level of mental organization, specifically at the level of the preconscious where "verbal ideas" emerge for the first time; the onset of the reality principle would coincide with the organism's need to understand its environment. But the reality principle can be said to arise because of external impediments to the satisfaction of drives—i.e., to internal stimuli—rather than because of merely external painful stimuli. The question might therefore be raised as to whether a cognitive drive would represent a later vicissitude of a more primitive drive (perhaps kept in place by anticathexes that might explain Kant's insistence on the unfathomability of the ultimate sources of cognition), or a more primordial drive to be posited at the level at which the unconscious forms "object ideas." However we answer this question—whether we posit an "originary" cognitive drive or view it as something developed out of the vicissitudes of other drives—we do not have to treat the desire to know as something caused by the reception of stimuli in sensibility. This is not to insist that the ultimate source of cognitive interest is internal as opposed to external, for things become complicated once we treat the inner/outer distinction as an unstable interpretation which inaugurates a subject-object mode of experience.

Where to fit a cognitive drive into a Freudian or postFreudian typology of drives will not concern me. Freud repeatedly indicates that he has no particular commitment to any particular set of drives; the fact that he revised his theory several times did not prevent him from retaining the basic contours of each discarded theory. For purposes of speculation, I will invoke the idea of a cognitive drive without worrying about whether it might be reduced to another drive, whether it should be defined with respect to the distinction between ego drives and object drives, with respect to the distinction between eros and the death drive, etc. In addition, the question as to whether the concept of a drive is ultimately as vacuous as the concept of opium's "soporific power" will prove to be of little concern.

Of more interest is the *function* of cognition, specifically the function of judgment. In his essay "Negation," Freud traces the origin of judgment to the organism's attempt to establish the inner/outer distinction: "The function of judgement is concerned in the main with two sorts of decisions. It affirms or disaffirms the possession by a thing of a particular attribute; and it asserts or disputes that a presentation has an existence in reality" (*SE* XIX, 236). Freud attributes the former task to the pleasure ego and the latter to the reality ego. In the first case, what is at issue is the organism's desire either to introject "good" objects and reject or project "bad" objects. In the second case, the ego performs the function of reality-testing, understood in the sense of distinguishing between merely inner hallucinations and genuinely external objects (*SE* XIX, 237). Thus, in both cases, cognition would arise as the fixing of topological boundaries.

That empirical cognition for Kant involves a regular movement back and forth between understanding and sensibility clearly parallels Freud's supposition of the rhythmic pulsation of an organism's feelers. On the

Kantian model, knowledge arises when this cycle is interrupted by an act of judgment. When the demand for knowledge is mitigated for some reason, the subject is said to experience pleasure from the free play of faculties that results (Kant's account of taste). In effect, we might suppose that the uninhibited organism would experience a free play of faculties (polymorphous perversity) until the demand for empirical cognition binds cathexes on to specific concepts for specific objects.

We can draw a further comparison between the distinction that Kant makes between empirical objects and the transcendental object and the distinction that Freud draws between the object of a drive and the aim of a drive. According to Kant, we cannot think an object of experience without positing the idea of its support—namely, "the non-empirical, that is, transcendental object = x" (A109). At the heart of Kant's refutation of idealism is his claim that I cannot have an experience of myself as being in time without my having an experience of an object that is outside of me: "inner experience is itself possible only mediately, and only through outer experience" (B277). Even though this outer object is merely empirical, and therefore an appearance, its existence guarantees the irreducibility of the thought of the transcendental object as that which marks the ultimate, if unknowable, reality of the object as a thing in itself. In other words, even though the refutation of empirical idealism does not establish that the objects which a subject intuits in space are outside it in a transcendental sense, it guarantees that empirical reality exists in some sense independently of the subject.

From the idea of the transcendental object, we get the idea of the thing in itself. However, Kant is careful to note that we should not confuse the negative sense of this idea—the idea of the noumenon—with any positive sense we might be tempted to give it:

> All our representations are, it is true, referred by the understanding to some object; and since appearances are nothing but representations, the understanding refers them to a *something*, as the object of sensible intuition. But this something, thus conceived, is only the transcendental object; and by that is meant a something = X, of which we know, and with the present constitution of our understanding can know, nothing whatsoever, but which, as a correlate of the unity of apperception, can serve only for the unity of the manifold in sensible intuition. (A250)

Of course, while Kant denies to the understanding the right to ascribe positive content to the transcendental object, he later both permits and does not permit reason to transgress the boundaries of the understanding (points to be taken up later).

What is ambiguous about the transcendental object is not merely the fact that it lies somewhere between the phenomena/noumena dichotomy. Like the subject of apperception, the transcendental object is nonphenomenal (i.e., an object of an infinite judgment). What is ambiguous is the fact that this nonphenomenal object both is and is not taken to be that about which we judge when we form judgments about empirical objects. On the one hand, we cannot formulate any judgments whatsoever about the transcendental object; like the subject of apperception, it is an empty "X." On the other hand, in judging empirical objects, we necessarily conjure the thought of the transcendental object as a pure indexical by which we refer to the noumenon as that which we would be judging were we capable of intuiting things in themselves. Thus, not only the fact that we cannot judge the noumenon, but the very idea of the noumenon, is indicated by a judgment that we formulate about the transcendental object—namely, the judgment that, whatever we ascribe to the empirical object is not a property of *it.* It is as if, "beneath" every affirmative judgment of an empirical object, there lurks an implied infinite judgment about the transcendental object. For example, "This chair (empirical object) is green" will carry with it the implied judgment, "This transcendental object is non-green." It is the consequent emptiness of the concept of the transcendental object that leads to the idea of the noumenon as that which we can think "only under the title of an unknown something" (A256/B312).

Thus, the transcendental object's nonidentity with the empirical object would seem to render all acts of judgment double. Or, more precisely, we could say that the spontaneity of the understanding refers all of its judgments about empirical objects to the concept of the transcendental object as that which, insofar as it cannot be judged, becomes reified as the thought of a thing in itself which escapes judgment. To the extent that this process gives rise to the idea of the noumenon, the understanding is led to "forget" that it is itself the author of the concept of the transcendental object in the first place (this is more or less Hegel's objection to Kant). The understanding then has the sense that all of its judgments "miss their mark," insofar as they do not arrive at the noumenon but apply only to empirical objects. This point is brought out by Žižek:

> what Kant fails to notice is that *das Ding* is a mirage invoked by the transcendental object. *Limitation precedes transcendence:* all that "actually exists" is the field of phenomena and its limitation, whereas *das Ding* is nothing but a phantasm which, subsequently, fills out the void of the transcendental object. (Žižek 1993, 37)

Understood in this way, the transcendental employment of the understanding would arise from an illusory "aim" that is just as spontaneous and captivating—and unsatisfied—as is the transcendent employment of the ideas of reason.

Freud's conception of the vicissitudes undergone by drives is relevant in this context. The aim of a drive is satisfaction, but insofar as external impediments prohibit such satisfaction, it is diverted from its "proper" aim. A diverted drive can take on a variety of possible trajectories, but all of them involve their being "cathected" or "attached" to a particular object.

Applying this model to the Kantian picture of understanding, we could speculate as follows. The understanding could be governed by a cognitive drive whose satisfaction would seem to be attainable only with the actual grasping of a thing in itself. The limitations of sensibility, however, function as external impediments which force the drive to be diverted on to empirical objects. Insofar as the empirical object is meant to be "the real thing," so to speak, the understanding conceives of it as a transcendental object, even though it knows that it cannot equate this object with a noumenal thing in itself. On this view, the spontaneous activity of the Kantian understanding could be thought of as a single process which both succeeds and fails to attain satisfaction.

We can refine this picture by relating it to Lacan's interpretation of Freud's theory of instinctual vicissitudes. According to Lacan, a drive is structured by the movement whereby an organism attains satisfaction precisely insofar as it fails to attain the object at which it aims (Lacan 1978, 179). Rather than view "impediments" to the drive as being merely external and accidental, Lacan takes the drive itself to posit the very impediments which will "force" it to veer from its ostensible destination. The "proper" object of the drive thus turns out to be entirely fictional; the true function of the drive is to fabricate an impossible object toward which the drive will move only in order to be turned back from it. Hence, the object of the drive "is in fact simply the presence of a hollow, a void, which can be occupied, Freud tells us, by any object, and whose agency we know only in the form of the lost object, the *petit a*" (Lacan 1978, 180). The object of the drive—the *objet petit a*—would be not the cause of the drive but its effect.

We can detect a similar structure at work in the Kantian cognitive drive. Its aim is to fabricate an impossible to attain transcendental object as that which the subject seeks to understand in order not to understand it. The place of this impossible object can be filled by any empirical object whatsoever, and the partial satisfaction of the drive would come from the understanding's ability to determine the nature of this empirical substitute-object. That the cognitive drive has nonetheless "succeeded" only by "failing" is evidenced by the fact that the empirical object is not the thing in itself that the transcendental object was meant to denote. The relationship between Kant's notions of the transcendental object and the thing in itself exactly correlate, as Žižek notes, to the Lacanian distinction between the *objet petit a* and the "Real" (Žižek 1993, 18). Just as, for Lacan, the lost "Real" is a fiction retroactively posited by the *objet a* which is supposed to compensate for this loss, so the Kantian noumenon is a fiction retroactively posited by the transcendental object. For Žižek, it is this retroactive positing which characterizes the act of symbolization:

> the transcendental object is the "in-itself" insofar as it is for the subject, posited by it; it is pure "positedness" of an indeterminate X. This "empty synthetic gesture"—which adds to the thing nothing positive, no new sensible feature, and yet, in its very capacity of an empty gesture, constitutes it, makes it into an object—is the act of *symbolization* in its most elementary form, at its zero-level. (Žižek 1993, 151)

From this, we could extrapolate that the Kantian cognitive drive is that which constitutes the Lacanian symbolic order—the order of phenomena—and simultaneously opens up the gap between the symbolic and the real. The analogue to Lacan's imaginary order could be located in those places where the understanding, instead of limiting itself to its immanent employment, tries to take on a transcendental employment, thereby lending itself to what Kant considers to be the illicit rule of the imagination. The understanding would be oriented toward the symbolic order, reason toward the order of the real, and the imagination toward the order of the imaginary.

By tracing what Kant calls the spontaneity of the understanding to a cognitive drive, I have so far limited my speculation to the most general feature of the activity of judgment—the circuitous path whereby it constitutes the empirical object as object of the drive in order to "go around" the object of desire, the transcendental object. On Kant's view, however, this general movement actually contains four distinct aspects, articulated in the four moments of quantity, quality, relation, and modality. Is Kant describing four moments of a single cognitive drive, or should we take his analysis as a clue that there may be four distinct drives at work? If the moments of judgment could be separated from one another—for instance, if we could form a judgment that had a modality but no relation—then we would have grounds for viewing them separately. But because every judgment has a certain quantity, quality, relation, and modality, it would seem to make more sense to treat these as aspects of a single cognitive drive.

On Kant's view, every judgment relates a concept to some other representation. The latter can be either a concept or an intuition, but if it is a concept, this concept must itself be related to an intuition:

> Judgment is therefore the mediate knowledge of an object, that is, the representation of a representation of it. In every judgment there is a concept which holds of many representations, and among them of a given representation that is immediately related to an object. (A68/B93)

By relating a concept to another representation, a judgment provides a function of unity to the representation in question. In order to deduce the moments involved in the activity of judging, it suffices to give a complete account of these functions of unity (A69/B94). Each of these functions will reflect the fact that a particular type of concept is employed in the act of judgment, and so from the moments of judgment we can deduce the fundamental types of categories that are at work in all spontaneous acts of the understanding. As functions of unity, the categories constitute the objective character of objects of intuitions; that is, these latter become objects insofar as they are thought through the categories.

Taking at face value Kant's fourfold tables with their tripartite subdivisions, can we relate this map of cognition to the logic of the drive? Following Reich, who convincingly shows that Kant presents his tables in synthetic rather than analytic order (Reich 1992, 62–63), we can start with the function of modality as that which introduces the objective character of the judgment. Modality would reflect the positing of the object of the drive as an object. Relation would reflect that in the object which we seek to know, and as such it could be said to constitute the understanding's movement toward the object. So, for example, modality might constitute as an existing object the dew on the grass, and the subject's seeking to articulate the causality behind this phenomenon would reflect the moment of relation. That the subject does not arrive at the thing in itself but only at the empirical object would be reflected in the fact that the judgment has a particular quality that is conditioned by the forms of intuition. Finally, the return of the drive—its satisfaction in the subject's having come to know the empirical object despite the fact that s/he has failed to grasp it as a thing in itself—would be reflected in the moment of quantity, which articulates the empirical scope of the subject's knowledge.

Relating this model to Freud's speculations concerning the origin of the ideas of time and space, we could present the following picture. Prompted by the "displeasure" of the cognitive drive, a projected object is posited as either actually, possibly, or necessarily existing in space. This object is thematized as something which is to be avoided, but also as something to be known. The rhythmic pulsation of perception, which gives us the concept of time, manifests itself in terms of a positing of a relation in the object which can be one of substantiality, causality, or reciprocity. Thus, we can draw a tentative parallel between the Kantian forms of intuition and the dynamic categories: modality would be the positing of an object's relation to space, and relation would be the positing of an object's relation to time (keeping in mind that both succession and simultaneity are temporal relations). Now, precisely because the object is a projected source of pain, the cognitive drive ultimately aims to avoid the object. But at the same time the ruse of projection requires that the object be treated as something real, and as the supposed aim of cognition. In this way, the cognitive drive constitutes a cognitive demand—the demand to know the projected object. We pass from demand to desire, however, at the level where it is the noumenal object that is at stake. This desire is both irreducible and unsatisfiable; the drive constitutes the conditions for the possibility of demand and the impossibility of desire. As part of the structure of the drive, cognitive demand manifests itself in the recognition of the quality of an object—whose degree of intensity might reflect the intensity of demand—and in the final act whereby judgment both seizes and fails to seize the nature of this quality through the moment of quantity.

Kant's claim that experience always consists of intuitions united with concepts can thus be traced to a unifying principle—the logic of the drive. Moreover, by tracing both the forms of intuition and the categories to a cognitive drive, we can also locate the place of desire within Kant's first *Critique.* That the spontaneity of the understanding can give rise to an unsatisfiable desire to know is suggested in the third *Critique* in the "Analytic of the Beautiful." The experience of aesthetic pleasure which we take in the contemplation of a beautiful object is directly connected with the fact that the cognitive drive never achieves what would seem to be its proper aim—namely, the determinate knowing of an object. This satisfaction, which Kant attributes to an a priori delight that we take in the free play of our faculties, is clearly related to a satisfaction beyond the satisfaction of cognitive desire. In Lacanian terms, then, we could say that cognitive *jouissance* is the *jouissance* of the drive, not of desire, and it is this that shows that the true aim of the cognitive drive is not to know the object that it posits. More precisely, translated back into Kantian terms, the transcendental object would be the object of the drive, the empirical object would be the object of demand, and the noumenal object would be the object of desire.

On this view, what Kant calls the spontaneity of the understanding always grafts the desire to know on to an empirical object of demand. While any empirical object can fill this requirement, not every empirical object will in fact arouse the interest of the understanding. The question of the arbitrariness of "object choice" here is analogous to the psychoanalytic question concerning "choice of perversion."

Freud defines perversion as the manifestation of a sexual impulse that separates itself from what would seem to be the proper aim of sexual activity—namely reproduction:

> The essence of the perversions lies not in the extension of the sexual aim, not in the replacement of the genitals, not even always in the variant choice of the object, but solely in the exclusiveness with which these deviations are carried out and as a result of which the sexual act serving the purpose of reproduction is put on one side. (*SE* XVI, 322)

What is both distinctive and paradoxical about a perversion, on this view, is that it represents a kind of autonomous deviation from that which sets it on its course. The aim of reproduction is put aside as the perversion manifests itself with an ulterior aim and an ulterior object. At the same time, Freud suggests that there is not necessarily anything "abnormal" about perversion; on the contrary, all human sexual activity might be said to contain an element of perversion: "some perverse trait or other is seldom absent from the sexual life of normal people." At most, the distinction between "normal" and "perverse" sexual behavior will be one only of degree, although Freud clearly wants to maintain some sort of distinction here: "There is no sense in excluding people with individual traits of this kind from the class of the normal and putting them among the perverts" (*SE* XVI, 322).

Not only can we borrow the concept of perversion in order to elucidate the structure of a cognitive drive, we can also explain the perversions themselves by thinking of them in terms of a drive to cognize reality. Lacan reads Freud, in fact, as accounting for "the approach of reality" in terms of a "desexualization" that masks cognition's erotic content (Lacan 1978, 155). In all perversions, something on the order of a transgression is at stake; the perverse subject goes beyond a "normal" limit or barrier of some sort (*SE* XV, 208). As Lacan shows in his reading of Kant and Sade, perversion represents desire in its "pure" form—i.e., stripped of any empirical object of demand (Lacan 1989, 67). We can suppose, then, that the perverse subject treats empirical objects not qua empirical objects but qua hidden, mysterious noumenal secrets which the perverse subject tries to extract. In this sense, the core of perversion would be an intensification of the cognitive drive.

Imagine the case of someone who can achieve sexual gratification only by smelling women's underwear. By attempting to know the nature of women's underwear—presumably the activity of smelling is synonymous here with the subtlest means of detecting a thing's essence—the subject would try to grasp that "X" whose seeming mystery is merely a reflection of its own illusory belief in the noumenal object. The desire to know the underwear-in-itself would reflect the relative autonomy that desire has come to have with respect to the cognitive drive which gives rise to it in the first place. Speaking of the voyeuristic gaze of the pervert, Lacan notes, "what he is trying to see . . . is the object as absence" (Lacan 1978, 182).

Whereas the neuroses, I have argued, represent purely aesthetic modes of space-time curvature, the perversions represent cognitive modes of space-time curvature. Just as the Rat Man must take every step necessary in order to return the money to the lieutenant, so here women's undergarments are objects that must be approached, looked at, smelled, touched, etc. But the Rat Man's duty was "mathematical" because what was of primary importance was not a particular fetishized object but the constant need to submit his actions to temporal laws. Here, the perverse subject's duty is "dynamical" because it concerns a particular fetishized object whose ultimate nature must be known. The "alchemical" moment of the perverse subject's experience occurs in the transformation of an arbitrary empirical object into a fetishized object. For at that moment—which Lacan explains in terms of the logic of the *point de capiton*—it is no longer the object qua empirical object of demand that is of interest but the object qua noumenal object of desire. Here too we see the paradox whereby the arbitrariness of object-choice turns a particular object into a mysterious fetish simply because it is whatever particular object it is—but qua transcendental object; Žižek gives a comparable analysis of the function of "the Jew" for the anti-Semite (Žižek 1993, 149). For the perverse subject who smells underwear, underwear is fascinating simply because it is what it is—namely, underwear. Of course, the object in question might not be an "original" object-choice; it could turn out that women's underwear is an object that has been metonymically substituted for some other fetishized object. Either way, the perverse subject's cognitive desire will have the same structure.

If my account is right, then the Kantian tables of judgments and categories present us with maps of the structures of possible perversions. In the next chapter, I will argue that Kant's so-called "principles of the understanding" in fact articulate rules of perversion-formation. Here I will simply stress a point already made with respect to the obsessional neurotic in the previous chapter—namely that the subject-who-judges will turn out to be a result, rather than the ground, of judgment. Therefore, rather than locate the source of a cognitive drive with the original synthetic activity of a unifying subject, as Kant does, we would have to explain the judging subject as something itself constituted by the drive. This means that the question concerning the "legitimacy" of the functions of understanding will give way to a question concerning the genesis of the distinction between the legitimate and the illegitimate, the normal and the perverse. Put otherwise, the burden of a metapsychological Analytic of Judgment would be not to provide a deduction of the necessary forms of experience but to speculate on the contingent character of cognitive perversions. Here the problem would manifest itself not only at the level of empirical object-choice (i.e., the question of which particular object will be fetishized), but also at the transcendental or quasitranscendental level where what is at issue is a question concerning the possibility of inventing new "types" of perversion. This is a question that bears on the ethics of psychoanalysis—in particular on the question of whether analysis should aim at adapting subjects to already given structures of experience or whether it should aim at the possibility of transforming such structures. I will return to this question in later chapters; here I will simply cite Lacan's hint at a negative answer to this "utopian" question:

> Perhaps we should give up the hope of any genuine innovation in the field of ethics—and to a certain extent one might say that a sign of this is to be found in the fact that, in spite of all our theoretical progress, we haven't even been able to create a single new perversion. (Lacan 1992, 14–15)

In this context, we can appreciate how suggestive Quine's analysis of "gavagai" talk is—but also how rigidly Kantian his solution to the problem is. Quine imagines a web of beliefs that would contain types of judgments radically different from those of "normal" subjects, but then he pulls back and maintains that no such radically different webs of beliefs are really possible at all. Perhaps the fact that we are always more likely to translate "gavagai" as "rabbit" rather than as "undetached rabbit part" or "rabbit time-slice" merely reflects the fact, as Hume would say, that we are creatures of habit. The possibility might nonetheless remain that a web of beliefs could be constructed very differently. The problem with articulating what it would be like to live in a world of time-slices rather than rabbits is that even a term such as "time-slice" is one which we automatically construe in terms of an ontology of objects that remain unified over time. This is why it so notoriously difficult to describe alternative "possible worlds" (though interesting attempts can be found—for instance in Borges's "Tlön, Uqbar, Orbis Tertius"). Perhaps by failing to take up the possibility of alternative conceptual perversions, Quine retreats from the potentially radical character of his ontological relativity thesis; it is certainly not surprising that he bases his argument on rhetorical invocations of the difference between "the normal" and "the abnormal." Likewise, the fact that Kant is describing the contours of a way of thinking which many of us—including Lacanians—happen to share might only serve to obscure the fact that his represents only one possible type of perversion.

# 4

# Principles of Discourse

> Understanding is not simple spontaneity arising over this passivity; it is subject to *forcing*. The great Kant overturned epistemological naturalism, biologism and pragmatism by declaring that the mind does not think because it has a natural tendency to think; on the contrary, as soon as there is the first movement of thought, thought finds itself under an imperative.
> —Lingis 1988, 135

> That my divisions in pure philosophy almost always turn out tripartite has aroused suspicion. Yet that is in the nature of the case.
> —Kant 1987, 38

> A quadripartite structure, given the unconscious, is always to be required in the construction of a subjective ordinance. Our didactic schemas satisfy this requirement.
> —Lacan 1989, 62

Up until this point there has been an ambiguity in my treatment of cognition as a drive. On the one hand, I have been relating Freud's account of the inner/outer distinction to Kant's distinction between time and space. On the other hand, I have been relating Freud's account to Kant's distinction between sensibility and understanding. This ambiguity is perhaps unavoidable. For while Kant certainly thematizes the difference between time and space as the difference between inner and outer intuition, he also treats both time and space together as forms of receptivity in contrast to the spontaneous activity of the understanding. Although time and space are themselves pure forms of intuition, the sensory manifold which appears in time and space is completely empirical and as such separate from the subject of apperception. All this is of course further complicated by the fact that everything phenomenal might in a transcendental sense be thought of as "on the side of" the subject; that which would lie "on the other side of" the subject remains unknowable. Of course, since that which might lie on the "other" side of the subject is (or includes) the subject as it is *in itself,* this distinction itself breaks down in some sense; it was for this reason that I argued against a "two-" or "three-self" reading of Kant's account of subjectivity.

Kant thus weaves a complicated web of intersecting divisions between what belongs to the subject and what does not. The distinction between objects of inner intuition and objects of outer intuition represents the division between the empirical subject and the rest of the empirical world. The distinction between sensibility and understanding represents a division within the subject between its receptivity to experience and its synthetic activity. Finally, the distinction between phenomena and noumena represents a division between the subject and itself.

These topographical complications find their parallels in Freud as well. In his first topography, Freud distinguishes between the different psychic systems of the unconscious, the preconscious, and consciousness. Overall, this model is analogous to the Kantian distinction between faculties. At first glance, the distinction between the unconscious as site of the drives and consciousness as the site of contact with the world might seem to correspond to Kant's distinction between the spontaneity of understanding and the receptivity of sensibility. If, however, the ultimate source of the drives lies (as I will argue) not with the understanding but with the imagination, then we could compare the unconscious to the imagination, the preconscious to the understanding, and consciousness to sensibility. Grouping the preconscious with the unconscious (as Kant, for example, subsumes the faculty of imagination under the faculty of understanding) would then give us Kant's distinction between understanding and sensibility. Alternatively, grouping the preconscious with consciousness—Freud calls attention to the structural ambiguity that allows for both possibilities (*SE* XIV, 189)—would give us more or less the same result, though it would raise certain problems.

Of course, Freud later complicates this picture with his presentation of the id, ego, superego model. Since the superego originally results from the introjection of sensory data originally taken to exist outside the ego—what Freud calls "preconscious verbal residues" (*SE* XIX, 52)—it reflects not only an intrasubjective distinction among separate agencies or faculties but also the distinction between the demands of the id and the demands of the external world. In this sense, the superego is a reaction-formation that marks the distinction between space as form of outer intuition and time as form of inner intuition. In other words, as Lacan's model of the mirror stage suggests, the subject would first appear as a "geometrical" subject; only with the introjections that will culminate in the development of the superego does it become a "temporal" subject. In keeping with my suggestion that obsessional neurosis manifests itself in terms of temporal symptoms, it is not surprising that the superego makes itself felt especially strongly in obsessional neurotics (*SE* XIX, 53).

Finally, Kant's distinction between the subject qua phenomenal and the subject qua noumenal finds its echo in Freud's insistence on the ultimate unfathomability of the unconscious.

In his "A Note upon the 'Mystic Writing-Pad,' " Freud presents a way of linking these seemingly disparate distinctions between the subject and its other:

> If we imagine one hand writing upon the surface of the Mystic Writing-Pad while another periodically raises its covering-sheet from the wax slab, we shall have a concrete representation of the way in which I tried to picture the functioning of the perceptual apparatus of our mind. (*SE* XIX, 232)

We have, on the one hand, a structural division between "faculties" reflected in the distinction between the wax slab, the transparent sheet of celluloid, and the thin sheet of waxed paper. On the other hand, we have a genetic account of the division between the apparatus as a whole and the writing that might be inscribed on it and erased from the top sheet.

The cognitive drive, I have suggested, will reflect a going-back-and-forth between sensibility and understanding. This is represented in Freud's model by the relationship between the periodic appearing and disappearing of the writing on the surface and the mnemic traces that are stored on the wax resin. Viewed from another angle, the cognitive drive can also be thought of as giving rise to the distinction between objects of inner sense and objects of outer sense. The idea of the external world—in the sense of objects in space—is occasioned by the fact that when the writing on the surface disappears it does not reappear. Thus, in his "Metapsychological Supplement to the Theory of Dreams," Freud notes that "A perception which is made to disappear by an action is recognized as external, as reality; where such an action makes no difference, the perception originates within the subject's own body—it is not real" (*SE* XIV, 232). Conversely, the idea of inner objects would arise from the possible return of an idea in memory—when the unconscious sends its writing back to the surface of the apparatus. As already indicated, it is in the cyclical movement from the unconscious to consciousness that Freud locates the origin of the idea of time.

Putting all this together, it would follow that the cognitive drive pulses between understanding and sensibility and that it is this pulsation which constitutes the distinction within sensibility between inner and outer objects of intuition. The back-and-forth between understanding and receptivity is then repeated as the back-and-forth within receptivity between objects of inner sense (e.g., in dream time) and objects of outer sense (e.g., reality-testing). All of this suggests, of course, that the concept of the body as limit will be necessarily ambiguous. This point is brought out in a letter sent by Lou Andreas-Salomé to Freud: "our body must play for us a double role, since it is just as much 'we ourselves' as also at the same time the most immediate piece of external reality" (Andreas-Salomé 1985, 25).

Working on the further assumption that the cognitive drive is experienced as something like an internal pain, both projection (origin of the idea of space) and the positing of an object of the drive (origin of the idea of the transcendental object) can be thought of as two aspects of a single process. Moreover, the cyclical process whereby the psychic apparatus approaches and withdraws from the external world (origin of the idea of time) is exactly homologous with the process whereby the drive posits (modality), seeks (relation), misses (quality), and returns from (quantity) a posited empirical object.

What Kant singles out as being most mysterious in experience is not the fact that we possess the forms of intuition and categories which we do, but the fact that we happen to map them on to each other in the particular way in which we do. We can supposedly notice the arbitrariness of the schemata in a way that we cannot recognize the arbitrary character of the forms of intuition or the categories. In the former case, it is possible to imagine how things might have been otherwise. Why, for instance, is the category of causality schematized by "the succession of the manifold, in so far as that succession is subject to a rule"? (A144/B183). In principle, this is a merely contingent fact. For all we know, the imagination could have schematized the category of causality in reference to, say, an *interrupted* succession subject to a rule. Had this been the case, the category of causality would have a different meaning: it would imply that there is always a delay between the occurrence of a cause and the occurrence of its effect. The mystery of the schematism, then, could be formulated as a question: Why do we imagine things one way rather than another?

On Kant's view, the pure forms of intuition and the categories are heterogeneous because they share no common trait (A137/B176). They become comparable only through a third element, provided by the imagination. The schemata therefore seem to play a secondary role, exactly on the order of what Freud identifies as the function of "secondary elaboration" in the dream work. They are created by the imagination in order to relate elements (concepts and intuitions) which otherwise would remain radically separate from each other—precisely in the way that secondary elaboration links unconscious drives to preconscious objects from which they are otherwise cut off.

But what if the work of imagination played a more fundamental role in constituting, rather than bridging, the division between concepts and intuitions? What if the schematism itself were the primary mechanism of the cognitive drive, the forms of intuition and the categories its derivatives? These are possibilities which Kant does not consider, but which are suggested, precisely, by the metapsychological decision to treat the synthetic a priori as analytic a posteriori.

The idea that imagination might lie at the root of cognition would be in keeping with Heidegger's reading of "the transcendental power of imagination . . . as the origin of pure, sensible intuition" (Heidegger 1990, 118)—leaving aside, for now, the question of whether from a metapsychological standpoint imagination would have to be thought of as empirical rather than transcendental. For Heidegger, imagination is not a secondary faculty whose activity is subordinate to the work of understanding; it is the primordial ground of the forms of intuition themselves. In fact, it is only after Kant pulls back from this insight that he himself relegates the imagination to a subordinate role in experience (Heidegger 1990, 112). Taking this suggestion one step further, perhaps what counts as cognition for Kant arises only by way of a repression of the constitutive work of imagination. At the level of the primary process, the role of imagination is evident; it functions as a faculty of hallucination. With the onset of the reality principle, imagination would be held in check. If this is so, then perhaps what I have been calling the cognitive drive would have to be thematized dynamically as a conflict between imaginative cathexes and discursive anticathexes. Concerning the schematism, Kant famously writes:

> The schematism of our understanding, in its application to appearances and their mere form, is an art concealed in the depths of the human soul, whose real modes of activity nature is hardly likely ever to allow us to discover, and to have open to our gaze. (A141/B180–81)

It is easy to read this as a prohibition of the form: "You must not because you can't!"—i.e., we ought not to plumb the depths of imagination because we can never fathom them anyway. Of course, basing an "ought not" on a "cannot" suggests something on the order of what Freud calls the "kettle logic" of dreams—i.e., it is an argument whose component parts undermine rather than support each other (*SE* IV, 119–20; *SE* VIII, 62, 205).

To the extent that the activity of the productive imagination is something of which we are not conscious, it can be called unconscious in the descriptive sense of this term. If we further take the imagination to be something actively repressed, then it would be unconscious in what Freud calls the dynamic sense of the term as well (*SE* XII, 261). Were we to trace the origin of the forms of intuition and the categories to the activity of the productive imagination, we could think of the entire quasitranscendental cognitive "crust"—including now not only space and time but also the forms of thought—as a kind of reaction-formation. As already mentioned, Freud takes the "crust" to protect the psychic apparatus from external stimuli. But insofar as the conditions for the possibility of experience limit what we can think, we can suppose that this crust also protects the ego from internal stimuli as well. Hence, we can think of the forms of thought as collectively playing the role of guardian of conscious life. Only those thoughts which meet the conditions for a possible experience are allowed to become conscious; other thought-impulses must be repressed. Prior to the formation of this crust, perhaps, the productive imagination has a limitless potential for thinking. Painful experiences lead it to restrict its free play, with the result that the understanding restricts its use to the production of a set of rules to govern its thought. These rules become reified, and so the resultant crust no longer seems to be a product of the imagination, but rather a fixed framework which imposes itself on the imagination. This process would parallel the manner in which the superego first appears through introjection and is then reified through a movement of projection (in the latter case, the belief in God).

According to Kant, the principles of understanding are synthetic a priori rules which articulate the necessary relationships between the categories and possible experience (A156/B195). If, however, the productive imagination gives rise to a particular set of "normal" manifest judgments only after repression, we could expect that the principles of the understanding are analytic a posteriori rather than synthetic a priori. Only because these products of the imagination are treated as if they cannot be altered would the ego view them as a priori. For this reason, it is not surprising to find that space, time, and Kant's so-called "laws" of thought do not hold in the unconscious: "There is nothing in the id that could be compared with negation; and we perceive with surprise an exception to the philosophical theorem that space and time are necessary forms of our mental acts" (*SE* XXII, 74).

If the conditions for the possibility of conscious experience turn out to be the conditions of repression, the neuroses and perversions would represent symptoms indicating a return of the repressed. Up until now, I have more or less treated the purely aesthetic neuroses and the cognitive perversions as two separate classes of phenomena. Without giving up this distinction, the homologous relation between intuitions and concepts suggests that neuroses and perversions are correlative aspects of the way in which the cognitive drive manifests itself. Every cognition involves an act of judgment which ascribes a concept to a represented object of intuition. What motivates the judgment is an internal thought-stimulus which, because it is painful, cannot be thought. However, by an act of projection, an external object is posited as that which consciousness takes to be provoking thought. Conforming to the structure of the internal thought-stimulus, which both must be thought and must be censored, this projected empirical object presents itself as something which can be thought (qua empirical object) and as something which cannot be thought (qua transcendental object). The psychic apparatus then goes out to and returns from this object, avoiding it under the pretense of approaching it. Perhaps the act of judgment is neurotic in that it posits an empirical object of demand which curves the subject's space and time, and it is perverse in that it derives its satisfaction from failing to attain its object of desire. As such, every cognitive experience will involve a relation between a neurosis and a perversion. Or, to paraphrase Kant, neuroses without perversions are dumb; perversions without neuroses are blind.

But this picture has to be complicated a bit. For Kant, the principles of the understanding are ways in which possible objects of outer intuition are submitted to temporal laws. In this sense, the principles could be said to submit hysterical symptoms to obsessional symptoms. The obsessional neurotic harbors fantasies of enactment, but does not act on these fantasies. Suppose perversion simply turned out to be the result of the enactment of the obsessional subject's fantasies. This would suggest a way of reading Lacan's "Kant with Sade." In this essay, Lacan presents two schemata, the first of which could be said to represent the (Kantian) obsessional neurotic's Sadean fantasy, and the second of which could be said to represent the perverse subject's enactment of this fantasy.

We can expect that all of Kant's principles of the understanding will exhibit a similar structure. They will exhibit a manifest level of "normal" discourse, supported by a repressed fantasy. Were the repressed fantasy to assume the position of the manifest discourse—not, I will suggest, by way of rotation but by inversion—we would then have an explicit perversion.

On this model, then, Kant's principles of the understanding would be structures which map possibilities of symptom-formation. As such, they can be expected to perform two functions: on the one hand, they will articulate the conditions for the appearance of obsessional and perverse symptoms, and, on the other hand, they will ground these conditions on the repression of a further spontaneity of the imagination. Put otherwise, the principles will ground conditions of possibility on the maintenance of conditions of impossibility.

Insofar as they promote (possible) symptoms and repress impermissible (impossible) thought-stimuli, the Kantian principles can be said to play a normative role in cognitive life. Of course, for Kant the sense of normativity here is limited to a purely cognitive "warning" that the understanding will veer into error if it tries to overstep its proper bounds. He does not think that the principles of the understanding are injunctions in the same sense that the categorical imperative is, perhaps partly because in the latter case, "ought" implies "might not" as much as it implies "can," whereas in the case of the principles, Kant maintains that it is simply not possible to think meaningful thoughts otherwise than in accordance with them. Hence, the prohibition against cognitive error (in the sense of the transcendental employment of the understanding) is not so much a prohibition against thinking certain things as it is a prohibition against taking pseudothinking to be genuine thinking. (In this respect, Kant of course anticipates the logical positivist credo.) Yet, at the same time, he does not merely take the principles to give us the means for distinguishing genuine thinking from pseudothinking, he construes them as *legislating* against pseudothinking. (In this respect, also, he anticipates the logical positivists.) Kant thereby conveys a sense that the principles impel us to censure bad metaphysics—the most egregious form of which would be what he repeatedly deplores as the *Schwärmerei* of anti-Enlightenment philosophers such as Hamann (which has curious affinities with the concept of amentia that Freud takes from Theodor Meynert) (*SE* XIX, 150).

Hence, the principles *compel* the understanding. If we think of the supposed spontaneity of the understanding in terms of the concept of the drive, we can attribute this sense of cognitive compunction to what Freud calls the dynamic dimension of psychic life. But from where would something on the order of a prohibition against cognition originate? Would this correlate with a shift from a cognitive "pleasure principle" to a cognitive "reality principle"?

To give a complete metapsychological account of the Kantian principles, we would have to articulate not only the "topographical" manner in which the various faculties of the quasitranscendental crust interact with each other in experience, along with the "economic" dimension by which the drive invests the principles with a certain force for both "discharging" cognitive excitations and for repelling the force of certain unconscious thought-stimuli, but also the dynamic process which is responsible for both cognitive symptom-formation and for the formation of topographical divisions in the first place.

Freud and Lacan suggest somewhat different models for thinking about the dynamic dimension. For Freud, the vicissitudes of drives are to be explained in terms of a conflict between the pleasure principle and the reality principle. For Lacan, as already indicated, there is no sharp division between a presumed "natural tendency" of a drive and its "contingent diversion"; built into his conception is the idea that the object of a drive is posited *in order* to be deviated from. Hence, the dynamics concern not a conflict between a cathexis that seeks to attain an object and an anticathexis that seeks to prevent the attaining of an object. Instead, the dynamics are internal to the drive itself. This kind of a model explains why it is in the end impossible to draw any kind of rigorous distinction, as Freud notes, between a "normal" development of a drive and a "perverse" deviation of it (*SE* VII, 171).

If the perversions in general can be said to represent enactments of the fantasies of obsessional neurotics, we nonetheless have to distinguish between mathematical and dynamical perversions. Kant's mathematical principles concern "the mere *intuition* of an appearance in general" (A160/B199), and as such they treat objects only insofar as these are represented in accordance with specific spatiotemporal neuroses. By contrast, the dynamical principles concern the *existence* of objects, and as such they involve the positing of an empirical object of a cognitive perversion.

Understood in discursive terms, each of the principles of the understanding could be said to impose a rule of speech on the subject—"You must say (or think) such-and-such when confronted with an object of intuition"—and at the same time a rule of silence—"You must not say (or think) such-and-such." The former would correspond to the moment of manifest symptom-formation, and the latter to the moment of repression. Hence, each of the four types of principles—the Axioms of Intuition, Anticipations of Perception, Analogies of Experience, and Postulates of Empirical Thought—would correspond to two types of discourse: a necessary discourse and a proscribed discourse. The necessary discourse would be the manifest content of a given principle, and the proscribed discourse would be its latent discourse. For every principle, the manifest discourse would function as a two-term relation between one of three categories of a given moment of judgment and an intuition. But "beneath" this discourse there would be the latent discourse which the manifest discourse is meant to repress. This latent discourse can also be represented as a two-term relation, but because it is something unthinkable, its form will be different from any of the forms which the manifest discourse takes. Strictly speaking, the unthought cannot be formulated at all; to the extent that it is articulated by the latent discourse, the latter will function as the representative of that repressed thought-stimulus which cannot be represented. Thus, we can equate the latent discourse with what Freud calls the representative of a repressed representation (*Vorstellungsrepräsentanz*). As we will see, the latent discourse of a particular manifest discourse will not belong to the same moment of judgment as the manifest discourse. Take, for instance, what would be the manifest discourse of the Axioms of Intuition, whose principle states: "All intuitions are extensive magnitudes" (B202). Here we would have a relation between a category of quantity and a possible intuition. In keeping with the logic of the drive, the category of quantity would represent not only the grasping of an empirical object but also the failure to grasp the object qua transcendental object. While the manifest discourse ascribes a quantity to an empirical object, the latent discourse is prevented from predicating something of the transcendental object. But what would this "something" be? A quantity? No, because quantity, a mathematical concept, can be predicated only of a spatiotemporal object. To grasp the transcendental object would be to attain that which the drive ostensibly sets out to know, namely the nature of the object as a thing in itself. In its transcendental employment the drive aims at the thing considered as a noumenal relation between unthinkable predicates, not as a quantity. Hence, the manifest discourse of quantity could be said to repress a latent discourse of relation.

In order to explain, I will ascribe markers to the four different "privileged" moments of the manifest discourses. Following Reich, I will continue to take the order of the categories and principles in reverse. Suppose we let $S_1$ stand for any of the categories of modality, $S_2$ for a category of relation, $ for a category of quality, and *a* for a category of quantity. These, of course, are the sigla which Lacan uses to play various roles in his schemata, and I have deliberately chosen them in order to show how we can draw a parallel between Lacan's four discourses (Lacan 1991a) and the four pairs of discourse that I take to be embodied in Kant's principles.

Unlike the other categories and schemata, those that belong under the heading of modality concern not features of objects per se; rather, they specify the relationship between an object of experience and the thinking subject. The modality of a judgment fixes upon a particular empirical object and declares it to be something which, for the subject thinking it, is either possible, actual, or necessary. For example, when Descartes raises the problem of skepticism in his First Meditation, he is considering whether more or less clear and distinct objects of thought are merely possible or genuinely actual. Significantly, it is only when he comes across an object which he takes to be necessary (God) that he becomes assured of the possibility of deciding whether a particular object is possible or actual.

We might schematize the formula of Cartesian objectivity as follows:

$$S_1 \rightarrow S_2$$

where $S_1$ represents the self-certain *cogito* and $S_2$ represents God. By extension, $S_2$ could also refer to any part of the objective world, insofar as its objectivity is guaranteed by the supposition that God is not a deceiver. Altogether, the formula would represent the basic structure of empirical knowledge. Such knowledge would be equivalent to metaphysical certainty, understood in the sense of a subject's ability to determine whether a particular object of cognition is possible, actual, or necessary. In other words, the basic form of Cartesian certainty would be given as the ability to make judgments of modality. Viewed from a psychoanalytic perspective, the Cartesian subject could be said to represent the fantasy of a scientific subject without an unconscious—hence the absence of anything appearing below the level of the manifest discourse.

In his rejection of the Cartesian model, Hume does not merely put us back in the position of the *cogito* raising its doubts about objects. Hume calls into question not only the subject's ability to ascertain the truth of judgments of modality, but also the very existence of the thinking subject. Accordingly, Hume's formula for cognition might be represented as follows:

$$\$ \rightarrow a$$

where $ would be the subject's recognition that it is completely ignorant of what—or even whether—it is and *a* would be the nature or source of impressions insofar as this remains completely mysterious. Of course, Hume also recognizes that for various reasons the subject becomes habituated to think of itself in Cartesian terms. Thus we could say that Hume calls attention to the following structure:

$$\frac{S_1}{\$} \rightarrow \frac{S_2}{a}$$

whereby the Cartesian fantasy is shown to be supported by its repressed epistemic support.

supposed spontaneity of the understanding can be understood in terms of a logic of the drive, then the empirical object will always be a projected surrogate for something that originates within the drive itself; more precisely, it will be the correlate of what is repressed in imagination. Insofar as the object is represented as something which must be known because it cannot be known, it exercises its fascination over the perverse subject as something which both entices and eludes cognition. Hence, it is the moment of quantity which corresponds to the representation of the transcendental object as *objet petit a*, for which reason I will denote it by Lacan's marker *a*.

Lacan identifies four types of discourse, each of which we can use to specify a particular relation between a manifest level of signification and a repressed level of signification. They are diagrammed as follows (Lacan 1991a):

| Master | University | Hysteric | Analyst |
|---|---|---|---|
| $\dfrac{S_1}{\$} \rightarrow \dfrac{S_2}{a}$ | $\dfrac{S_2}{S_1} \rightarrow \dfrac{a}{\$}$ | $\dfrac{\$}{a} \rightarrow \dfrac{S_1}{S_2}$ | $\dfrac{a}{S_2} \rightarrow \dfrac{\$}{S_1}$ |

In each of these cases, the upper left-hand term functions as the defining feature of the discourse; the master is defined by $S_1$, the university by $S_2$, the hysteric by $, and the analyst by *a*, for reasons which I will go into. For now, I will associate each of the Lacanian discourses with its corresponding Kantian pair of principles:

| Master | University | Hysteric | Analyst |
|---|---|---|---|
| Modality | Relation | Quality | Quantity |

The top half of each discourse would represent a manifest judgment. On the left would be the operative moment of judgment, and on the right would be the object of the judgment. The object's character will vary in accordance with the different moments of judgment that are ascribed to it. So, for example, in the discourse of modality, the object will appear as $S_2$, while in the discourse of relation, it will appear as *objet a*. What is being predicated of the object is what is on the left-hand side. Thus, we could say that each moment of judgment discursively characterizes an object that is presented as already having been "worked over" by another moment. For instance, the moment of modality will predicate a category of modality ($S_1$) of an object that is already given as a relation ($S_2$). This is in keeping with the fact that judgments link signifier to signifier; a judgment refers a signifier (concept) to an object of intuition only insofar as another signifier has already stood in for that object.

As for the bottom halves of the schemata, these would represent the repressed discourses. Lacan takes the discourse of the master, for example, to repress what he defines as the formula of fantasy, $\$ \Diamond a$. If we were to read this as $\$ \rightarrow a$, we could say that we have here a form of judgment that is not sanctioned by Kant. For it would appear to be a judgment of quality, since $ is in the discursive position, but its object would be an object of quantity (*a*) rather than, as in the manifest discourse of quality, an object of modality ($S_1$). The fact that such a judgment would be literally unthinkable for Kant suggests that we can call it a judgment only in what he would call the problematic sense of this term. Instead of writing this repressed discourse as $\$ \rightarrow a$, we might make use of Lacan's little diamond—the sigla $\Diamond$—to indicate that we are referring to something that is a judgment in a different sense from what we take a judgment to be at the level of manifest discourse.

Lacan refers to the diamond in the formula $\$ \Diamond a$ as a "rim" (*bord*), a term which is also important for his analysis of the drive (Lacan 1978, 209). The rim is, essentially, a *limit* appearing precisely at the sites of the various inner/outer dichotomies. The aim of the drive is to go beyond this limit, from which it makes a circular return around the *objet a.* This suggests that we might read the moment of modality as determined by a moment of the drive that remains repressed. In fact, we can generalize Lacan's schemata of the four discourses by supposing that the drive will manifest itself in terms of four distinct moments. Taking the bottom half of each of the moments of discourse, we could write:

$$\$ \Diamond a \qquad S_1 \Diamond \$ \qquad a \Diamond S_2 \qquad S_2 \Diamond S_1$$

to indicate the four determining moments of the drive. This would suggest that the manifest discourse of a particular moment of judgment might be the compromise-formation that arises from the repressed aspect of the cognitive drive. If we take the left side of each of these partial schemata to represent the determining aspect of the drive, we could then associate each of the manifest discourses with its corresponding moment of the drive as follows:

| | | | | |
|---|---|---|---|---|
| Manifest Discourse: | Modality | Relation | Quality | Quantity |
| Moment of Drive: | Quality | Modality | Quantity | Relation |

Each of the manifest discourses would reflect the repression of the drive of *another* discourse. Translating back into Lacanian terminology, the discourse of the master represses the drive of the hysteric, the discourse of the university represses the drive of the master, the discourse of the hysteric represses the drive of the analyst, and the discourse of the analyst represses the drive of the university. But the relation of repression here is ambiguous, because that which is repressed functions as the fantasmatic support for the repressing manifest discourse. Specifically, the repression of the moments of the drive is the condition for the possibility of the emergence of that quasitranscendental "crust" which appears in the guise of Kant's four manifest moments of judgment.

To see how all this works, we need to examine Kant's four principles. I will start with the Postulates of Empirical Thought. Corresponding to the three moments of modality, there are three such postulates:

> 1. That which agrees with the formal conditions of experience, that is, with the conditions of intuition and of concepts, is *possible.*
>
> 2. That which is bound up with the material conditions of experience, that is, with sensation, is *actual.*
>
> 3. That which in its connection with the actual is determined in accordance with universal conditions of experience, is (that is, exists as) *necessary.* (A218/B265–66)

If the moment of modality can be expressed in terms of the top half of Lacan's discourse of the master, then all three of these postulates would represent a variant of the formula $S_1 \rightarrow S_2$. Now, we can treat $S_2$ as the object that is being judged to be either possible, existent, or necessary. Since $S_2$ corresponds to the discourse of relation, we would say that here $S_2$ refers to the object of relation. Hence the formula $S_1 \rightarrow S_2$ says that a moment of modality is applied to an object of relation. In other words, when we judge an object to be possible, existing, or necessary, we already take this object to be a relation of some sort. It is always a substance, a causality, or a reciprocity to which we ascribe a modality. Let me try to illustrate with reference to the dialectic of demand and desire. For any given empirical object, a subject might decide whether this object is a possible object of sexual demand (the question of object-choice), an actual object of sexual demand (immediate arousal), or a necessary object of sexual demand (fetish). But in order to be an object of sexual demand, the object must already be represented as something intrinsically *desirable* (application of the concept of substance), as something that happens to instigate desire in the subject (causality), or as something whose existence as desirable object is directly connected with the desirability of another object.

But the entire schema of modality says more. It says that the supposed spontaneity whereby the understanding ascribes a modality to an object of relation rests upon a repression of that aspect of the cognitive drive which can be associated with the moment of quality. Specifically, the formula $\$ \Diamond a$ represents a repressed judgment that applies a category of quality to an object of quantity. Now, since the manifest judgment of quality always takes an object of modality, this repressed judgment cannot be made conscious. Why? If we look at its structure, the formula $\$ \Diamond a$ says that a quality is applied to the object of quantity, insofar as this object is conceived in terms of the transcendental object. Obviously, for Kant, no category of quality whatsoever can be predicated of the transcendental object, for we can say neither that this object is nor that it is not. The formula $\$ \Diamond a$ represents a "fantasy" in the sense that what sustains the cognitive drive is the illusion that the transcendental object can in fact be known in terms of the categories of quality. It is this fantasy which sustains the modal judgment, whereby an object of relation is posited in the order of empirical reality. This is why Lacan says that "reality" is supported by the structure of fantasy.

In the last chapter, I suggested that the categories of modality would concern an object's relationship to space. That might have seemed to suggest an affinity between modality and hysteria. As already suggested, however, the Kantian principles represent perverse enactments of obsessional fantasies.

Lacan suggests that obsessional neurosis can be said to be supported by the fantasy of "Woman." Perversion can be equated with the attempt to *enact* the fantasy that Woman—the object qua transcendental object—is that which exists beyond the phenomenal veil presented by objects of experience. Here it is important to note that any existential reference to the "beyond" of experience will invoke this fantasy; that is, to take Woman to be the object of an affirmative, negative, or infinite judgment is to invoke the fantasy. For this reason, when Lacan crosses out the "*la*" in "*la femme,*" he does so not so as to be able to say that "Woman does not exist" (which would be to participate in the fantasy), but in order to call attention to the fantasmatic character of any existential judgment about Woman whatsoever (Lacan 1985, 149ff.).

In judgments of modality, objects in space are posited only insofar as they exist with respect to the judging subject. The fact that judgments of modality are supported by the repressed fantasy of Woman also suggests why, from an obsessional standpoint, hysteria is associated with femininity, and mastery— i.e., obsessional neurosis—with masculinity. Thus, we find categories of gender appearing for the first time from the standpoint of the obsessional subject. This is a point to which I will return in subsequent chapters.

For now, I turn to the Analogies of Experience. Again, Kant posits three:

> In all change of appearances substance is permanent; its quantum is neither increased nor diminished. (B224)
>
> All alterations take place in conformity with the law of the connection of cause and effect. (B232)
>
> All substances, in so far as they can be perceived to coexist in space, are in thoroughgoing reciprocity. (B256)

Each of these analogies gives expression to the manifest formula $S_2 \rightarrow a$. This says that the object of quantity—the transcendental object—is always judged as a relation. This, in fact, is precisely Kant's point. Unlike the case of Lacan's formula of fantasy, where the transcendental object would have to be treated in a way which is literally unthinkable, here the transcendental object is conceived in what Kant takes to be the only possible thinkable way. The fact that the analogies express dynamical principles means that appearances themselves, not merely our intuitions of them, must be shown to stand in relation to one another. Thus, Kant finds himself in the strange position of having to talk about an "appearance itself" (A191/B236). He can do so only by treating appearances as transcendental objects. This is why the "Refutation of Idealism," though it ostensibly concerns only a demonstration of the truth of empirical realism, nonetheless seems to support a certain minimal transcendental realist thesis. It makes sense, then, to say that the categories of relation are applied to objects of quantity.

What the manifest discourse of relation represses, however, is expressed in the schema $S_1 \diamond \$$. This says that the supposed spontaneity whereby the understanding ascribes a relation to an object of quantity rests upon a repression of that aspect of the cognitive drive which can be associated with the moment of modality. More precisely, the formula $S_1 \diamond \$$ could be said to represent a repressed judgment that applies a category of modality to an object of quality. The object of quality is the empirical object insofar as it manifests itself as the gap separating itself from the transcendental object. The categories of modality cannot be applied to this gap, and hence the formula $S_1 \diamond \$$ represents something that is unthinkable. Nonetheless, the ability to conceive of the transcendental object as a relation might be said to rest on the fantasy that we can give a positive sense to the transcendental object by taking the gap within the empirical object to be something that actually exists rather than something merely problematically conceived. Thus, the conditions for the possibility of this manifest discourse can be said to rest on both the possibility and the impossibility of the repressed judgment in question.

Once again, we might illustrate this by way of the logic of repressed fantasy. If we take the gap within the empirical object to represent the idea of the castrated mother, then what gets repressed is the possibility of treating the *lack* of the phallus as either possible, existing, or necessary. For Freud, of course, the trauma of the discovery that the mother lacks a phallus plays an important role in the development of various neurotic symptoms. So long as the fantasy of the phallic mother remains repressed, the subject remains at the level of a neurosis, but when this repressed fantasy itself becomes manifest there appears a structure of perversion. The basic moment of the logic of perversion here would find expression in the different ways in which a substitute for the mother's phallus is posited as the object that the subject attempts to cognize in terms of the concepts of substance, cause, or reciprocity.

So far I have examined the two dynamical moments of judgment. Because their manifest discourses require that a categorial synthesis be projected outward as a connection obtaining among the objects of experience themselves, they must presuppose—while repressing—a fantasy of the objective reality of the transcendental object. Thus, the objects of the two repressed discourses indicate the transcendental object, either directly (the *objet a* of modality's repressed judgment of quality) or indirectly (the $ of relation's repressed judgment of modality). We can expect that the mathematical moments of judgment will rest on repressed cognitive fantasies of a different sort.

According to Kant, the categories of quality find expression in a single principle which gives rise to the Anticipations of Perception: "In all appearances, the real that is an object of sensation has intensive magnitude, that is, a degree" (B207). This principle can be expressed by the manifest discourse $ → $S_1$. This says that in all judgments that arise out of the supposed spontaneity of the understanding, a category of quality is applied to an object of modality. Keeping in mind that, when we take the categories in reverse order we are developing them, as Reich shows, in an analytic manner rather than a synthetic manner, it is to be expected that the Anticipations of Perception are applicable to objects that are already determined as being possible, actual, or necessary. Examining the principle, we see that what it implicitly says is that every *possible* object of experience, if it were to appear as *actually existing* or as *necessarily existing*, would have an intensive magnitude.

But the principle of the Anticipations of Perception also rests upon a repressed fantasy that is expressed by the formula $a \diamond S_2$. By itself, this formula suggests a repressed judgment that applies a category of quantity to an object of relation. Kant himself gives us reason for saying that a category of quantity is applicable only to an object of quality. For only objects that are intensive magnitudes can collectively have an extensive magnitude. Were we to apply a category of quantity to an object of relation, we would be treating an object without any intensive magnitude—for neither the relations of substantiality nor causality nor reciprocity is revealed through sensation—as if it were something that had a sensible extent. Here it is important to notice that while according to Kant we must ascribe both a quantity and a relation to every object of experience, we do not apply these moments to the object considered in one and the same respect. What we ascribe a quantity to is an object of quality, not an object of relation, despite the fact that every particular object of experience will be an object of quality, an object of relation, and so on.

Looking now at the entire schema of the moment of quality, what it suggests is that the manifest discourse of quality presupposes the repressed fantasy that it is possible to determine an object of relation in accordance with a category of quantity. To see why this might be so, we should bear in mind that there is something paradoxical about treating an object of modality as if it could be determined by a category of quality. The Anticipations of Perception supposedly allow us to determine a priori a mere object of modality with respect to an aspect of its sensible quality, despite the facts that the material of sensation is a posteriori, and the object of modality is given a priori. Kant himself calls attention to this peculiarity: "The anticipation of perception must always, however, appear somewhat strange to anyone trained in transcendental reflection, and to any student of nature who by such teaching has been trained to circumspection" (A175/B217). Kant thinks he can solve the problem by noting that it is not the actual quality of sensation which we anticipate a priori but only the fact that any real quality will have a certain degree that is greater than degree 0 (A175–76/B217–18). But this argument still presupposes that the object of modality must have a degree of intensity, an assumption that would make sense only if it were possible to treat the object of modality as if it were an object of relation determined by a category of quantity. That is, if we could conceive of relations themselves as subject to judgments of extensive magnitude, then the fact that we treat all relations as subject to the categories of modality would provide a mediating link enabling us to ascribe a quality a priori to an object of modality. In fact, we cannot treat relations as having extensive magnitudes. Thus, the manifest discourse of quality rests on something repressed.

For both of the mathematical principles, the logic of the neuroses can again provide us with illustrations. In the case of the moment of quality, we can turn to the phenomenon of hysteria *as it is represented from the standpoint of the obsessional subject.* In hysterical neuroses, Freud argues, a repressed drive manifests itself through the appearance of some sort of somatic symptom. One characteristic of hysteria—unlike other psychoneuroses—is the fact that it involves a circumventing of consciousness. That is, a repressed drive does not pass directly from the unconscious to the preconscious-consciousness system; it bypasses the latter, manifesting itself in a somatic condition. Now, for the hysteric, the symptom will appear only as an object of outer intuition. But the hysteric's symptoms will appear to the obsessional subject as objects of inner intuition. Hence, the obsessional will speculate on the causes of the hysteric's symptoms—precisely as Freud does in the cases of Dora and the famous "female homosexual." For the obsessional analyst, the hysteric's symptoms will be classified as possible (as in anxiety hysteria), existing (as in conversion hysteria, where the fact that the symptom is actually present relieves the subject of anxiety), or necessary (as in the case of phobia, where anxiety returns because the symptom is now both present and impending). To judge with respect to a symptom would be to affirm, deny, or infinitely deflect (*détourner* might be a Lacanian equivalent)—i.e., to *interpret*—this object of modality. Herein, accordingly, would lie the manifest level at which the obsessional subject analyzes hysterical symptoms.

But all this would be possible only insofar as the manifest symptom—i.e., the desire of the analyst—results from the repression of a sexual drive. Now, if we take a sexual drive to take as its object a sexual relation, then it would make sense to expect that an object of relation is what is repressed. More precisely, it is the very possibility of treating either all sexual relations, a particular sexual relation, or some sexual relations as possible objects of judgment that is repressed in the obsessional subject's fascination with the hysteric.

Turning finally to the Axioms of Intuition, which articulate the rules for the application of the categories of quantity, Kant expresses these too in terms of a single rule: "All intuitions are extensive magnitudes" (B202). He adds, "I entitle a magnitude extensive when the representation of the parts makes possible, and therefore necessarily precedes, the representation of the whole" (A162/B203). From this it should follow that a judgment concerning an extensive magnitude ranges over objects which have already been represented as intensive magnitudes. In this sense, the categories of quantity would be applicable to objects of quality. This principle is accordingly given by the formula $a \rightarrow \$$.

Of all possible psychological types, the obsessional neurotic comes closest to representing what a normal subject would be. This is because "well-adjusted" functional subjects tend to be those with strong superegos, and those with strong superegos tend toward being obsessive. At the level of the manifest discourse, the principle of quantity indicates that objects which have already been affirmed, negated, or infinitely deflected can be judged collectively (subsumed under the categories of either unity or plurality) or individually. The manifest discourse might be said to represent the reality principle, insofar as it expresses that the subject exists qua judge in relation to objects whose essence is to be judgable. The obsessive component would be connected with the degree to which the subject feels compelled to judge objects. All "normal" subjects make judgments; an obsessional neurotic is someone who feels he or she must judge everything.

According to Freud, obsessional neurosis gives expression to a hostile impulse. Leaving aside the question as to whether aggression is to be traced to sexual drives, ego drives, or a death drive, it is clearly connected with the formation of the superego. This suggests that it is the fact that the subject has identified with someone that has judged it and is now as a consequence judging itself, that it has established itself as a judge of other objects. In other words, lurking beneath the ego's claim to be entitled to judge others is the fact that it is secretly judging itself all the while. The bottom half of the complete schema for the moment of quantity, $S_2 \diamond S_1$, would represent a formula for the structure of unconscious guilt. On the side of the subject is the introjected but repressed big Other; on the side of the judged object is the subject itself. This is why, when the obsessional subject's repressed fantasy is made manifest, it appears as the equivalent of Sadean perversion.

In each of these discourses, we notice that the four sigla perform different functions, depending on whether they represent *categories* being applied to objects or *objects* already subsumed by categories. The *objet a*, for example, is a category of the moment of quantity and an object of the moment of quantity. As a category, it signifies the concept of an extensive magnitude; as an object, it signifies the transcendental object. But these are correlative aspects of a single movement, for it is the application of the concept of extensive magnitude to an object which presents the object to be subsumed under a moment of quantity, and so on. Significantly, it is only in the two dynamical discourses that the transcendental object (*objet a*) appears qua object. In the mathematical discourses of quality and quantity, the *objet a* appears on the discursive side (in the repressed and manifest discourses, respectively).

Understood in the way I have described them, Kant's principles of the understanding mutually determine and limit one another. The manifest discourse that characterizes a particular moment of judgment finds expression in a particular principle or set of principles. These principles are applied to possible objects only insofar as these objects have already been determined by other principles, which in turn presuppose the application of other principles, and so on. This metonymic structure illustrates Lacan's conception of *signifiance.* For Lacan, the "bar" that separates a signifier from a signified is one that can never be crossed; the two belong to "distinct orders separated initially by a barrier resisting signification" (Lacan 1977, 149). Accordingly, signification—understood as a signifier's relationship to its signified—never quite takes place. What takes place in *signifiance* is the relating of one purported signification to other purported significations:

> No signification can be sustained other than by reference to another signification. . . . If we try to grasp in language the constitution of the object, we cannot fail to notice that this constitution is to be found only at the level of the concept. (Lacan 1977, 150)

The Kantian categories, I am arguing, function in precisely this way: they purport to be applicable to objects of intuition only insofar as other categories purport to be applicable to these objects, but in the end there is nothing that grounds this slippery slope. The empirical object always eludes cognition.

From all this I propose several conclusions. First, Kant's principles provide limiting conditions for the possibility of experience only insofar as they are "illegitimate," for the repressed judgments on which they rest are invalidated by the principles themselves. Thus, on merely coherentist grounds we would have to say that the *quid juris* question of the Transcendental Deduction receives a negative answer. Second, the concept of the transcendental object is revealed to be a cognitive symptom, not a metaphysical problem. Third, however, something analogous to the phenomena/noumena distinction remains as a problem, for although the problem of the transcendental object disappears, the problem of the ontology of the drive remains. As already indicated, the repressed fantasy is not identical to the unthinkable thought-stimulus; it is, rather, the *Vorstellungsrepräsentanz* of the drive. To this extent, metapsychology finds itself invoking the concept of the drive "itself" in a problematic way. As a result, it is likely that all the problems of metaphysics which arise at the level of Kant's "Dialectic" will resurface as problems of metapsychology.

In some sense, this result confirms Freud's dream of converting the problems of metaphysics into problems of metapsychology. But it also suggests that metapsychology, no less than metaphysics, can give rise to dialectical illusions.

If the principles of the understanding are illegitimate, they cannot represent synthetic a priori knowledge. Yet, each carries with it the sense of necessity, which suggests that the understanding posits an analytic connection between the subject and predicate of each of the principles. Kant, of course, maintains that the principles cannot be analytic because we could not, for instance, derive the concept of causality merely from the concept of alteration; only by relating our concepts to possible intuitions can we establish this connection. But this view presupposes the priority of forms of intuition and concepts over the schemata of imagination. If, as I have argued, intuitions and concepts are two moments of the cognitive drive, and if the schemata logically precede the division between the two, then each of the categories could be said to already "contain"—or better, reciprocally imply—that aspect of the form of time to which it corresponds. On this view, the applicability of a category to a certain possible intuition will be analytically derivable from the concept itself. The fact that empirical objects remain the condition for the possibility of this analyticity suggests that they function as if they were both analytic and a posteriori.

Having delineated the principles in what he takes to be an exhaustive and sufficient manner, Kant introduces his famous metaphor of the island surrounded by a sea:

> We have now not merely explored the territory of pure understanding, and carefully surveyed every part of it, but have also measured its extent, and assigned to everything in its rightful place. This domain is an island, enclosed by nature itself within unalterable limits. It is the land of truth—enchanting name!—surrounded by a wide and stormy ocean, the native home of illusion, where many a fog bank and many a swiftly melting iceberg give the deceptive appearance of farther shores, deluding the adventurous seafarer ever anew with empty hopes, and engaging him in enterprises which he can never abandon and yet is unable to carry to completion. (A235–36/B294–95)

While Kant claims to be a cautious seafarer, well aware of the deceptive appearances of the stormy ocean, he is so confident of his abilities as land-surveyor that he never once doubts whether he has charted the territory of his island accurately and completely. This island has definite boundaries: one can tell where its land ends and where the sea around it begins. If we imagine Kant's island having a more or less rectangular shape, its four sides—corresponding to the four principles of the understanding—would all be distinguishable from one another.

But if, as I have argued, the principles of the understanding ultimately rest upon perversions of themselves, it will turn out that the topology of Kant's island is more complicated. Perhaps we can think of it as a sort of projective plane. A projective plane is the geometrical figure that would result if we could take a sheet of paper and connect both of its opposite edges after giving one of each pair a half-twist. If we think of each edge of the paper as representing a principle of the understanding, and the half-twist as representing the "perversion" of the principle, we can think of the connection between any two edges as representing the subordination of one principle to its repressed fantasy. In order to apply this image more accurately, however, we would have to imagine that we could now connect the two connected edges. This would result in a figure which would represent the interlaced manner in which each principle both depends on another perverted principle and itself supplies its own perversion for another principle. We now have a picture of Kant's island.

Two questions immediately arise. First, is it possible to chart a single complete map of such an island? Or can we imagine alternative maps? Second, is it possible to delineate the boundaries that separate the island from its surrounding environment? Does the island have an "inside" and an "outside"?

One thing to notice is that, at the "seam" where all four edges meet, we have the basic structure of a judgment. If we now set out to chart its territory, we can set out along the path of, say, one principle, and find ourselves back at the seam. From there, we can set out along a second principle, and so on, until we have traversed the land in its entirety. This, more or less, is Kant's path. Alternatively, however, we could chart the same land in terms of the perversions of the principles, a process which would traverse the entire territory but yield a different map. It is important to keep in mind that a projective plane, like a Moebius strip, has only one surface. Therefore, what seem like mountains in one direction can seem like valleys in the other. Which bumps we take to be valleys and which we take to be mountains will depend, in effect, on whether we take our journey to be following the principles or following the perversions of the principles. Put in Kantian language, the "bumps" on our island will function like antinomies, and to this extent they may be as much sources of illusion as the fog-banks and icebergs at sea. That we may be in no better position "on land" than "at sea" leads to the further question of whether we can even be sure of the boundaries that supposedly separate the inside of the island from its outside. (Lacan's mitre and "interior 8" illustrate this same situation.) Since the topology of the understanding is itself antinomical, the categories are problematic even with regard to their claim to empirical validity. With the boundary separating empirical knowledge from noumenal speculation undercut, it is no longer the concept of the noumenon that turns out to be problematic, but the very distinctions between phenomena and noumena, sensibility and understanding, time and space.

The dialectical illusions of reason, which follow from the principles of the Kantian understanding, now take on a different character. For Kant, reason tempts the understanding to take its objectively valid principles and extend them beyond the limits of their proper employment. If, however, the principles themselves are judged to be antinomical, then the speculative tendency of reason will seek not to extend these principles but to explain them. Thus, all of the metaphysical speculations concerning the structure of reality give way to metapsychological speculations concerning the structure of the psychic apparatus. Kant's questions concerning the paralogisms, antinomies, and ideal of reason will all reappear under the guise of metapsychological, rather than metaphysical, questions—but in a double sense. On the one hand, there is the task of examining Kant's Transcendental Dialectic from the standpoint of metapsychology. On the other hand, there is the additional task of examining the dialectical problems that arise precisely within metapsychology itself.

Before turning to the problems of his Transcendental Dialectic, Kant indicates a peculiar class of issues that he lists under the heading of "Amphibolies of Reflection." Kant here introduces the idea of a "transcendental topic" (*Topik*: the same term that Freud uses to refer to what in English is rendered as "topography"). It is precisely at this point, in fact, that Kant comes closest to recognizing the need for the kind of metapsychological speculation that Freud will eventually introduce. On Kant's view, the transcendental topic has the role of "distinguishing the cognitive faculty to which in each case the concepts [of reflection] properly belong," an operation that "will provide a sure safeguard against the surreptitious employment of pure understanding and the delusions which arise therefrom" (A268/B324). Without the safeguard of a transcendental topic, he warns, we are liable to make the mistake of thinking in terms of illegitimate amphibolies:

> In the absence of such reflection, the use of these concepts is very unsafe, giving birth to alleged synthetic principles, which the critical reason cannot recognise, and which are based on nothing better than a transcendental amphiboly, that is, a confounding of an object of pure understanding with appearance. (A269–70/B325–26)

Kant goes on to criticize various Leibnizian doctrines which he claims arise from just such confusions. The general charge in each case is that Leibniz tried to create "an *intellectual system of the world*" by treating appearances as if they themselves were pure objects of the understanding (A270/B326).

Yet, Kant himself might be accused of succumbing to amphibolies, by falsely subsuming the faculty of imagination under the faculty of understanding. It is this error in particular that leads him to treat the analytic a posteriori as if it were synthetic a priori. At bottom, Kant's Transcendental Analytic does nothing more than reify a particular cognitive perversion—what we could call "an *intellectual system of nature.*" The difference between the truth-claims of natural science and those of speculative theology can no longer be drawn in any meaningful way—except, perhaps, as the difference between the metaphysics of perversion and the metaphysics of psychosis.

5

# Paralogisms of Narcissism

In conformity with these ideas as principles we shall, *first*, in psychology, under the guidance of inner experience, connect all the appearances, all the actions and receptivity of our mind, *as if* the mind were a simple substance.
—Kant 1965, A672/B700

In this respect, I cannot compare the soul more properly to any thing than to a republic or commonwealth, in which the several members are united by the reciprocal ties of government and subordination, and give rise to other persons, who propagate the same republic in the incessant changes of its parts.
—Hume 1978, 261

Kant's principles of the understanding, I have argued, can be said to enact perverse fantasies that remain unconscious for the obsessional subject. That they remain unconscious would signify that they are not allowed to go beyond certain limits. Specifically, the repressed fantasies are not allowed to enter consciousness. At the level of manifest judgment, however, this barrier to consciousness is represented under the form of "limits of experience." That is, the principles of the understanding specify the limits beyond which the enactment of perverse fantasy cannot go. These limits represent the obsessional refusal of a free play of the imagination.

At the level of the Kantian understanding, therefore, a dynamic tension is set up. So long as repression is maintained, the understanding does not allow the imagination to constitute judgments that go beyond the limits of experience. Taking a cue from Freud, however, we can suppose that there are limits to repression itself. At regular intervals, the imagination will violate these limits of experience, positing judgments that are ordinarily censored by the understanding. Herein lies the shift from understanding to reason, for Kant interprets reason as that faculty which possesses principles that bid the understanding to go beyond its proper limits: "I mean actual principles which incite us to tear down all those boundary-fences and to seize possession of an entirely new domain which recognises no limits of demarcation" (A296/B352).

Should we suppose, then, that the understanding represents a containment of perversion and that reason represents the release of perversion? This, for reasons I will explain more fully in the next chapter, would be too hasty. For what emerges at the level of reason—specifically with the antinomies—is a full-blown conflict between the hysterical and the obsessional moments of neurosis. My hypothesis will be that it is only with the reassertion of the dominance of the obsessional moment of judgment that Kantian reason can be said to renew the work of repression undertaken at the level of the understanding. But at that point, reason represents neither an obsessional neurosis nor a perversion, but rather a psychosis.

If the neuroses and perversions constitute structures of experience, what exceed these structures are the psychoses. As Freud treats them, schizophrenia and paranoia represent the two major forms of psychosis; in chapters 6 and 7 I will explain why schizophrenia should perhaps not be thought of as a psychosis. Here, I will focus on a phenomenon that functions as a kind of a "pivot" upon which the swing from neurosis to psychosis can take place: narcissism.

According to Kant, the "paralogisms of reason" are synthetic a priori judgments which give rise to the illusion that the subject can know what it is as a thing in itself—specifically, know itself as a simple, unitary substance that is in relation to possible objects in space (A344/B402). The paralogisms make the mistake of treating the subject as if it were an object. The category of substance is applicable only to objects which appear as permanent in time; it is not applicable to the subject for the simple reason that there is nothing permanent in thinking (A350).

Insofar as the paralogisms treat objects of experience as merely possible rather than as actual, they could be said to exhibit a narcissistic "withdrawal of cognitive libido" from the world. Kant argues that the paralogisms are specious because they go beyond the limits of possible experience, purporting to demonstrate the existence of something that can never be an object of knowledge. Lacking reference to any actual appearance (*Erscheinung*), the paralogisms can merely conjure an illusory object (*Schein*).

As critic of the idealistic claims of rational psychology, Kant could be said to carry out a critique of narcissism. This critique would be like that of the ego psychologist, for both seek to curb the pretensions of a megalomaniacal subjectivity while preserving the authority of the "normal" *cogito.* Thus, Kant insists that the spontaneity of the understanding must be attributed to the work of the subject of apperception:

> We now come to a concept which was not included in the general list of transcendental concepts but which must yet be counted as belonging to that list, without, however, in the least altering it or declaring it defective. This is the concept or, if the term be preferred, the judgment, "I think." As is easily seen, this is the vehicle of all concepts, and therefore also of transcendental concepts, and so is always included in the conceiving of these latter, and is itself transcendental. (A341/B399)

As critic not only of the paralogisms but of all the metaphysical pretensions which arise in the Transcendental Dialectic, Kant might seem to play the role of the "normal" analyst. As already indicated, Freud treats neurotic and perverse subjects as similar to "normal" subjects; it is only when he gets to psychotics that he finds subjects who appear to him to be truly abnormal. To this extent, it would not be surprising to find Kant constituting neurotic and perverse structures of experience at the level of the Analytic and then undermining psychotic structures at the level of the Dialectic. From such a perspective, Kant perhaps would never leave the level of the obsessional neurotic who harbors perverse fantasies but has no tendency toward psychosis proper.

This interpretation, however, might lay too much stress on the "negative" results of the Transcendental Dialectic, for Kant ultimately insists that it is his duty to believe in each of the objects of the ideas of reason. For example, having called attention to the spurious character of rationalist attempts to prove the existence of the soul, Kant immediately adds, "Yet nothing is thereby lost as regards the right, nay, the necessity of postulating a future life in accordance with the principles of the practical employment of reason" (B424). Kant thereby maintains a sharp distinction between an illusion (*Schein*) of "normal" reason and a delusion (*Wahn*) of deranged reason; he appeals to "the common reason of men" (*gemeine Menschenvernunft*) in order to warrant his continued belief in the existence of the soul (B424).

Thus, Kant's Dialectic does not have a merely negative role to carry out. The "discipline" of reason is supplemented by a safeguarding of reason's metaphysical pretensions; indeed, the objects censured as metaphysical illusions in the first Critique come back to haunt the Kantian subject with a vengeance in the second Critique. One way of reading this tension might be in terms of a struggle between a loss of reality and an attempt to reconstruct reality, a struggle which Freud takes to be typical of the onset of psychosis. In this sense, Kant's Dialectic would perhaps hover between obsessional neurosis and psychosis.

Reason constructs its ideas, Kant claims, by attempting to think the unconditioned first term for each series of conditions posited by the categories of relation. These ideas, though necessary, present the subject with no object of cognition: "Although a purely transcendental idea is, in accordance with the original laws of reason, a quite necessary product of reason, its object, it may yet be said, is something of which we have no concept" (A338/B396). Although the ideas present reason with no determinate objects, they do have a regulative employment: "namely, that of directing the understanding towards a certain goal upon which the routes marked out by all its rules converge, as upon their point of intersection" (A644/B672). It is important to notice, moreover, that it is not merely the ideas qua ideas which are at work here; it is the *imagined but inconceivable objects given through these ideas* that play a regulative role:

> Hence arises the illusion that the lines have their source in a real object lying outside the field of empirically possible knowledge—just as objects reflected in a mirror are seen as behind it. Nevertheless this illusion (which need not, however, be allowed to deceive us) is indispensably necessary if we are to direct the understanding beyond every given experience (as part of the sum of possible experience), and thereby to secure its greatest possible extension, just as, in the case of mirror-vision, the illusion involved is indispensably necessary if, besides the objects which lie before our eyes, we are also to see those which lie at a distance behind our back. (A644–45/B672–73)

This is why eventually, for Kant, we must—and the form of this *must* is complicated—believe in the existence of the objects of the ideas. The necessity of doing so is expressed in Kant's famous "as if" (*als ob*) formula concerning the idea of God: "The ideal of the supreme being is nothing but a *regulative principle* of reason, which directs us to look upon all connection in the world *as if* it originated from an all-sufficient necessary cause" (A619/B647).

The nature of the "as if" or "as if X" (where X is a judgment) is important to clarify. The cognitive attitude "as if X" is not a counterfactual, because the possibility remains that X might in fact be true. More precisely, X is a judgment whose truth or falsity can in principle never be determined by us. But it is precisely here that the difference between treating an *idea* as regulative and treating the *object* of an idea as regulative becomes important. If it were the idea alone that played a regulative role then we might say that the "as if" concerned the subject's acting as if he or she believed in the existence of a fictional object. But since, for Kant, it is the object of the idea that plays a regulative role, the "as if" seems to concern the subject's acting as if the object actually existed.

To illustrate the difference I have in mind, consider the case of parents who invoke regulative ideas whose objects they do not themselves believe in. A parent might tell a child that "the tooth fairy" exists. This need not be to not act as if the tooth fairy exists; it can be to act as if one believed that the tooth fairy existed. Some parents will try to get their children to believe that the tooth fairy actually exists; others will try to get their children to do what they themselves are doing—i.e., pretending to believe. In the latter case, they do not want their children to think that there actually is a tooth fairy in either a constitutive or in a regulative sense; they simply want their children to participate in the type of imaginative play which calls attention to its own playful character by invoking an "acting as if believing" in opposition to what we might call "acting as if knowing." In the latter case, the force of the "as if" is carried over to the object—i.e., we act as if the judgment X were true. In the former case, the phrase "as if" is applied to the believing itself rather than to its object—i.e., we act as if we believed that X were true.

All of this might seem like splitting hairs, but it is precisely such splitting of hairs that for Freud distinguishes the neurotic from the psychotic. As already indicated, both the neurotic and the psychotic are said to undergo a certain type of "loss of reality" (*SE* XIX, 183). This loss bespeaks a topographical regression which we could characterize as the retreat from the authority of the understanding back to a limited free play of the imagination. Something of this sort could be said to take place at the level of Kant's Transcendental Dialectic, where reason gives rise to concepts of objects which, strictly speaking, are possible only given a suspension of the "censorship" of the understanding. Here it is worth recalling that reason's violation of the principles of the understanding is said to pose legitimate problems, whereas the understanding's violation of these principles is said to give rise only to error.

It would be important to distinguish between that "primary" free play of imagination which would precede the formation of fixed schemata and the "secondary" work of imagination which takes place only by way of a violation of the established rules of such schemata. The former would correspond to the activity of hallucination associated with the primary process. The latter would correspond to an activity of illusion-formation associated with a struggle between the ego and the repressed drive. The best model for this is given in the case of schizophrenia, which Freud takes to exhibit a struggle between the subject's loss of reality and its subsequent attempt to "recover" its loss. Such a struggle might be said to appear in the conflict between Kant's treatment of the ideas as illusions and his treatment of them as giving us objects we must believe in. Ultimately, perhaps, the "discipline" of reason counts as a redoubling of the work of repression, one carried out at the conscious level rather than the unconscious level.

But this suggests that the illusions of reason might indicate not a renewed free play of imagination but on the contrary a strengthening of the censorship of the understanding. It is important to remember that the roots of Kant's metaphysical illusions might be located back at the level of the Analytic. By limiting the scope of cognition to appearances, he could be said to have left open too wide a domain for the free play of the imagination (the sphere of things in themselves). The ideas of reason could then be thought of as delusional stop-gaps designed to prevent hallucination (Kant's struggle against *Schwärmerei*). By reducing the objects of experience to mere appearances, he had already in effect prepared the very sort of "end of the world" which Freud associates not with the neurotic but with the psychotic (*SE* XII, 70).

Perhaps we can put all of this together by interpreting the Kantian dialectic as follows. First the imagination posits an idea which violates the rules of the understanding. Second—precisely through the critique of the "illusions" posited by the imagination—the ideas are "reworked" so as to *serve* the work of the understanding. This would explain why Kant interprets the "as if" formula as requiring an "acting as if knowing"—for what supposedly counts merely as a regulative idea in fact plays a kind of surreptitious constitutive role.

The first step taken in both neurosis and psychosis concerns a turning away from something painful in reality and the establishing of a "world of phantasy" (*SE* XIX, 187). This imaginary world functions as a kind of substitute for the reality that the subject wishes to avoid. In neurosis, the subject continues to acknowledge the force of reality, and therefore acknowledges that its imaginary substitute world is simply a fantasy. By contrast, the psychotic denies aspects of reality altogether, attempting to reconstruct portions of the world on the basis of its fantasy. Freud characterizes the difference as follows: "Neurosis does not disavow the reality, it only ignores it; psychosis disavows it, and tries to replace it" (*SE* XIX, 185). The neurotic, in short, acts as if he or she believed in the fantasy world without actually believing in it, while the psychotic believes in the fantasy world as if he or she knew that it existed.

Because he construes the regulative employment of the transcendental ideas as requiring an "acting as if knowing," Kant has a difficult time showing in precisely what sense he means to call the objects of the ideas illusions. He also finds himself repeatedly trying to strengthen the so-called regulative requirements of reason so that in the end the subject can be said to regain metaphysical knowledge from the standpoint of the demands of practical reason. It is not that Kant waffles on this point. He simply draws the logical consequences that follow if reason demands "acting as if knowing" rather than "acting as if believing." Reason, it turns out, demands the onset of psychosis.

Kant gives his most striking description of this demand in the passage that I cited in the first chapter, where he indicates that "nothing can shake" his belief in God:

> I inevitably [*unausbleiblich*] believe in the existence of God and in a future life, and I am certain that nothing can shake this belief, since my moral principles would thereby be themselves overthrown, and I cannot disclaim them without becoming abhorrent in my own eyes. (A828/B856)

Kant here seems to depart from a major tenet of the Cartesian tradition by invoking the notion of a belief that can be necessary without counting as knowledge; in this respect, he anticipates the cognitive attitude of the Kierkegaardian knight of faith. When he says "nothing can shake this belief" he does not mean this in a merely psychological (i.e., pathological) sense; yet neither does he mean this to indicate something on the order of dogmatic certainty. He is invoking something like "transcendental indubitability" as opposed to either empirical or metaphysical indubitability. Of course, even if we were to grant Kant his claim to identify the moral facts and regulative demands of reason, it would still seem that the most he could establish would be the necessity of "acting as if believing" rather than "acting as if knowing" unless, that is, what is at work here is the experience of the psychotic.

The ideas are said to force themselves on the subject when reason tries to take the Analogies of Experience to their logical conclusion. Kant maintains that the objects of the ideas are illusory because they purport to go beyond the boundaries determined by the principles of the understanding. But if the principles are themselves as ill-founded as any of the pseudoproofs which reason will develop, it is possible that dialectical illusion arises not from the fact that reason takes the principles "too far," but simply because reason makes explicit the cognitive fantasies that the principles presuppose. The chief difference between the principles and the dialectic of reason would be that the imaginative character of the categories remains repressed, while the ideas—at least as Kant analyzes them—wear their imaginative character on their sleeves. Or, put in topographical terms, we could say that the understanding is where the work of repression takes place, and reason is the site of a return of the repressed. That is, the ideas irrupt at the level of reason because of a failure of repression at the level of the understanding. At the moment where the ideas emerge in consciousness with all their hallucinatory force, reason would mark a regression to the level of the imagination—and of a return of the hysterical moment which previously had been made subordinate to the obsessional laws of inner sense. Is it any surprise, then, that Kant invokes the metaphor of a mirror image in order to explain the appearance of the ideas?

What, then, is the relationship between the irruption of the repressed and reason's subsequent attempt to discipline itself? As Freud points out, both psychoanalysis and psychosis begin from the task of bringing the repressed into the open; he notes in this connection the striking parallels between the delusions of psychotics and the explanations of these delusions which psychoanalysis proposes. Lacan similarly refers to the tendency of psychosis to "virtually theorize" itself: "We also find in the very text of the delusion a truth that isn't hidden, as it is in the neuroses, but made well and truly explicit and virtually theorized" (Lacan 1993, 28). Part of the explanation for the parallel between psychosis and psychoanalytic theory, Freud suggests, is that psychosis frequently exhibits an attempt at a "cure." Such an effort can be detected in Kant's attempt to expose the delusions of metaphysics. By insisting on the cognitive limits posited by the understanding, Kant maintains the value of what counts as "reality," but he does this while simultaneously allowing the imagination a certain restricted free play.

The entire Kantian dialectic of reason might be described on this model. Each pseudorational "proof" of the existence of an object of a transcendental idea could be viewed as a manifest discourse which gives expression to a repressed fantasy. By revealing the fantasy in each case and by demonstrating its illegitimacy, Kant develops a full-blown critique of reason's tendency to allow the imagination its free play. At the same time, by arguing for the necessity of acting as if knowing that the objects of the ideas did exist, he allows for a sort of compromise-formation between the imagination and the understanding.

Helene Deutsch invokes the concept of an "as if" personality type in order to explain certain forms of schizophrenia. In doing so, she says that her use of the "as if" should not be associated with the Kantian-influenced "as if" philosophy of Hans Vaihinger. According to Deutsch, an "as if" person is someone "whose relationship to life has something about it which is lacking in genuineness and yet outwardly runs along 'as if' it were complete" (Deutsch 1965, 263). Specifically, the person lacks any genuine object cathexis, with the result that he or she is "attached" to nothing, and only passively adopts the affective attitudes of others (Deutsch 1965, 265). It is easy to see why Deutsch would distinguish between this personality type and the cognitive attitude recommended by Vaihinger's philosophy of fictions. As in the case of Kant, Vaihinger's "as if" invokes the logic of "acting as if knowing." The personality described by Deutsch, by contrast, seems to suggest an "acting as if believing."

Here we can see the difference between the ideology of a cynical reason and the critical distance of irony. Whereas "normal" subjects might cynically act as if they knew their (empirical) ontological assumptions were correct, Deutsch's "as if" personality ironically acts only as if he or she believed in such assumptions. Surprisingly, however, Deutsch does not detect anything of therapeutic value about such irony. She finds herself uncertain as to whether or not the "as if" personality should be classified as a psychotic, noting that the retention of "reality-testing" skills distinguishes the "as if" person from a true psychotic (Deutsch 1965, 278). Thus, she suggests that the "as if" personality tends toward being delusional—a conclusion one would expect her not to make given her account of the difference between the "as if" type and a Vaihingerian personality. Without discriminating between types of identification, Deutsch assumes that an "as if" patient who identifies with a dog is necessarily acting in a delusional manner (Deutsch 1965, 279). Here, I would invoke Deleuze and Guattari's discussion of "animal-becomings" to suggest that what might be at stake with the "as if" type is a subversive subjectivity perhaps not unlike their conception of a "schizo" (Deleuze and Guattari 1987, 233ff.).

At any rate, Deutsch's "as if" personality seems to indicate a subject who recognizes that the principles of his or her understanding are themselves fictions. This recognition leads the subject to perform an "as if" epoché, thereby opening up the potential for a free play of imagination that violates conventional principles of understanding. Naturally, such a person will be judged "abnormal" by those so-called "normal" subjects who insist upon the dominant cognitive fantasies of the social groups to which they belong. It is noteworthy in this context that Deutsch never suggests that her "as if" patients see *themselves* as sufferers; her only evidence that there is "something wrong with them" comes from the fact that "normal" people find them to be strange:

> Even the layman sooner or later inquires, after meeting such an "as if" patient: what *is* wrong with him, or her? Outwardly the person seems normal. There is nothing to suggest any kind of disorder, behavior is not unusual, intellectual abilities appear unimpaired, emotional expressions are well ordered and appropriate. But despite all this, something

intangible and indefinable obtrudes between the person and his fellows and invariably gives rise to the question, "What is wrong?" (Deutsch 1965, 263)

Deutsch's approach seems to typify what Deleuze and Guattari object to as the psychoanalytic practice of submitting schizos to "normalizing" judgments. If we take their concept of "Oedipalization" to refer to the process whereby a subject comes to accept a social group's dominant principles of understanding, then we can read Deleuze and Guattari as objecting to a process that would teach subjects to unlearn their ability to imagine the world being otherwise than they are taught to construct it.

Perhaps the opening for critique in general is made possible by an initial "as if" epoché, which can then develop either in the direction of a liberating of the imagination (such as Kant undertakes to a limited extent in the third Critique), or a paranoid foreclosure of the work of critique (such as Kant develops in the second Critique). Can we detect a similar problematic within metapsychology? A "constitutive" metapsychology would be one that dogmatically posited the objects of its ontology; a "regulative" metapsychology would treat its ontology as problematic. But here too we might distinguish between two sorts of regulative metapsychology—"cynical" and "ironic." Deleuze and Guattari, while nonetheless making use of certain metapsychological concepts, suggest that psychoanalysis has become a sort of cynical practice. This would be so in a double sense: first, insofar as its therapeutic ideal has become a conformist one; second, insofar as it gives rise to a dogmatic ontology of its own. To illustrate the latter point, they call attention to various "paralogisms" of psychoanalysis. In each case, what is at issue is a certain "transcendent use of the syntheses of the unconscious" (Deleuze and Guattari 1983, 73).

As Kant notes, the paralogisms of the soul appear to be synthetic a priori truths that can be deduced syllogistically from the mere idea of a thinking subject. The error consists in the fallacious assumption that what holds for the logical subject of thought must also hold for the subject that appears in intuition: "The logical exposition of thought in general has been mistaken for a metaphysical determination of the object" (B409). Similarly, in metapsychology, a series of paralogisms of the unconscious that appear to be synthetic a priori truths can be deduced from the idea of a thinking subject. The difference is that, for Kant, the subject of thought is the subject who makes synthetic a priori truths possible; for the metapsychologist, the subject of thought would be the subject who makes analytic a posteriori judgments possible. In effect, the metapsychologist asks for the conditions for the possibility of a subject who treats a posteriori judgments as if they were analytic, and comes up with the answer that such a subject must be unconscious.

Understood in this way, a series of paralogisms of the unconscious might be mapped as negations of Kant's paralogisms of the soul as follows:

1. The unconscious is not a substance.
2. It is not simple. 3. It is not a unity.
4. It is in relation to impossible objects.

Because the subject's judgments violate the laws of logic, as Freud repeatedly emphasizes, it cannot be simple (the fact that it contradicts itself implies that it is divided), it cannot be a unity (for it is not simple), and its objects must be impossible (for they are the objects of contradictory judgments). Thus, we see the unconscious described in terms of three of the four moments of judgment. Most important, though, is the fourth moment—the moment of modality—which Kant takes to be the starting point of rational psychology's positing of the soul. Metapsychology does not classify the unconscious as a substance. The question is whether it thereby treats the unconscious as the object of a negative judgment or as the nonobject of an infinite judgment.

To say that the unconscious is *nonsubstantial* would be to resist giving it any fixed ontological status. This, I take it, is the point to be emphasized in Lacan's treatment of the unconscious. As the object of an infinite judgment, the unconscious escapes Kant's phenomena/noumena dichotomy. Recall the projective plane metaphor invoked in the last chapter, which suggests that the "line" of cognition is nonorientable. On the one hand, the unconscious is said to lie "behind" the manifestations of the cognitive drive as something that remains repressed ("the other side of experience"), while at the same time manifesting itself as that which gets repressed in the first place and as the return of the repressed ("this side of experience"). Understood in this way, the unconscious both appears and does not appear, an ambiguity that precisely corresponds to the nonphenomenal (but not noumenal) character of the "I think." This suggests a fuller response to Kitcher: the reason why the subject does not fit into the phenomena/noumena dichotomy is that the question of its location is topographical rather than ontological.

The idea of approaching the unconscious from a topographical rather than an ontological standpoint is, of course, at the heart of Lacan's enterprise. In this sense, Lacan is to Freud what Kant is to Leibniz. By arguing that the unconscious can be understood only in terms of a logic of the signifier, Lacan introduces as a regulative principle the claim that no ontological status can be assigned to the unconscious whatsoever. What counts as a signifier is always a "surface" element; any illusion of noumenal depth is rejected. Lacan thematizes this as an insistence on a certain type of "naturalism":

> I will only add that the maintenance of this aspect of Freudianism, which is often described as naturalism, seems to be indispensable, for it is one of the few attempts, if not the only one, to embody psychical reality without substantifying it. (Lacan 1978, 72)

But can a naturalistic attitude avoid the problems of ontology altogether? Because he does not treat the unconscious as a substance, Lacan believes that he is not reifying it. However, treating something as a substance is not the only way of reifying it; the application of any category of relation to the unconscious would count as reification.

The key claim of Lacan's metapsychology is that the unconscious is structured like a language. On this view, the unconscious is differential—it is a network of signifiers which stand in reciprocal relation to one another. So long as we keep the concept of the differential open—as in the case of Derrida's *différance*—this is not in itself an ontological statement. The problem arises when we treat the differential in terms of the closed concept of *structure*, for the concept of structure is the concept of a multiplicity of terms existing in a relation of reciprocal determination—i.e., it is the Kantian category of community.

Kant derives the category of community from the form of the disjunctive judgment. In a disjunctive judgment, a group of objects is judged as a whole that is divided up into parts that mutually determine one another. Unlike the parts of a hierarchically determined whole, which are represented as standing in a relation of subordination to one another, the parts of a disjunctive whole are represented as standing in reciprocity with one another:

> Since no one of [these parts] can be contained under any other, they are thought as co-ordinated with, not subordinated to, each other, and so as determining each other, not in one direction only, as in a series, but reciprocally, as in an aggregate—if one member of the division is posited, all the rest are excluded, and conversely. (B112)

To be sure, Kant generally conceives of community in terms of a reciprocity of self-identical substances, whereas structuralism posits a reciprocity of signifiers that are what they are only in relation to one another. But this is not as significant a difference as it might seem, because we can think of structuralism as simply treating accidents rather than substances as standing in reciprocal determination with one another. In rejecting the substantification of the unconscious in favor of the concept of structure, Lacan could be said to shift attention away from one category of relation to another. We could thus attribute to Lacan the following four paralogisms:

1. The unconscious is a community.
2. It is divided. 3. It is a plurality.
4. It is in relation to impossible objects.

If we subsume the concept of structure under the concept of totality, then Lacan's claim that the unconscious is not a substance will not be an infinite judgment. It will be a negative judgment for which we can immediately substitute the affirmative judgment that the unconscious is a community. But Lacan goes back and forth on these matters, and one can find places where he treats metonymy, for example, as implying the radically open-ended character of the differential. Unlike Leibniz, who envisioned the possibility of a *mathesis universalis,* Lacan treats his diagrams and graphs as so many props not to be taken too seriously: "Be careful! They are supports for your thought that are not without artifice, but there is no topology that does not have to be supported by some artifice" (Lacan 1978, 209). Here we find the ironic Lacan for whom the "paralogisms" would themselves function merely as imaginative supports of metapsychological speculation.

The diagram given above corresponds to Kant's synthetic grouping of the paralogisms of the soul. Corresponding to Kant's analytic table (B419), we would then have, for Lacan:

1. $ thinks,
2. as "it" separate from "I," 3. as "I" separate from "it,"
4. as non-identical subject in every state of my thought.

The "I think" is translated into "$ thinks" to indicate that the subject of thought is always other than the "I" that speaks. The second and third moments are expressed by Lacan in his account of how Freudian theory transforms the Cartesian *cogito.* As Žižek notes, Lacan offers different readings of this transformation (Žižek 1993, 59). On one presentation, Lacan suggests that for Freud the self-awareness of the conscious subject establishes that there is thinking, but the doubt which sustains the *cogito* indicates that the I that sees itself and the I that thinks are not equivalent (Lacan 1978, 36). On this view, Descartes's "I think, therefore I am" can be written as "I am, therefore it thinks," where the "it" (*ça; Es*) would represent that part of the subject which is other than the I which is self-conscious. Alternatively, one might write, "I think, therefore it is," to indicate that it is the thinking of the conscious ego which establishes the existence of the unconscious subject. Žižek rightly points out that both of these moments are structurally implied in Lacan's view, for the barred subject is always split with regard to its being and its thinking. The "I" which thinks (subject of the enunciation) and the "I" which is said to be (subject of the enunciated statement) are not identical. If the subject is located on the side of thought, then it is not where it thinks; if it is located on the side of being, then it does not think where it is:

> In the span of three years, Lacan elaborated two opposed readings of the *cogito*. In both cases, he broke up the unity of *cogito ergo sum*: *cogito* is conceived of as the result of the forced choice between thought and being, i.e., "I am not where I think." (Žižek 1993, 59)

As Žižek shows, the choice between "I think, therefore it is" and "I am, therefore it thinks" reflects a structural necessity of the barred subject, rather than merely an uncertainty in Lacan's mind about which way to characterize his view. Both of these positions, expressed in the second and third paralogisms above, are mutually antagonistic—a conflict which will resurface at the level of the antinomies. These two paralogisms give expression to the communal reciprocity which the first paralogism takes the subject to be. That is, the barred subject is a community to the extent that if it thinks, then it is where it does not think; and if it is, then something thinks in its place. Or, as Lacan elsewhere puts it: "I think where I am not, therefore I am where I do not think" (Lacan 1977, 166).

The fourth paralogism explicitly brings together these two moments to amplify what is implied in the first—namely, that the barred subject who thinks is always other than itself. What this means, put in Kantian terminology, is that both an "I think" and an "It thinks" must be able to accompany all my representations. Strictly speaking, however, we can no more conclude from the thought of the barred subject that the unconscious exists as a community than we could conclude from the ego's perception of the unity of consciousness that the soul exists as a substance.

Žižek goes one step further and takes the choice between the two positions to represent the choice of sexual identity. This is a point I will take up more explicitly in the next chapter. Here, I will simply note that the split between being and thinking—i.e., the split between femininity and masculinity—coincides with the split between the hysterical subject of space and the obsessional subject of time. In other words, "I think, therefore it is" represents the masculine obsessional subject in relation to the feminine subject ("I think, therefore Woman is"), and "I am, therefore it thinks" represents the feminine hysterical subject in relation to the masculine subject ("I am, therefore Father thinks"). Whether the antinomies that result from this conflict require solutions or not will be seen to bear on the structure of schizophrenia.

6

# Antinomies of Schizophrenia

> If philosophy now and then reminds us of such schizophrenic behaviour, that not only speaks against philosophy, but a bit also for schizophrenia.
> —Andreas-Salomé 1985, 41–42

> When we think in abstractions there is a danger that we may neglect the relations of words to unconscious thing-presentations, and it must be confessed that the expression and content of our philosophizing then begins to acquire an unwelcome resemblance to the mode of operation of schizophrenics.
> —Freud *SE* XIV, 204

For Kant, the idea of the world as totality—and its dynamical corollary, the idea of nature—are regulative concepts that guide reason in its empirical employment. Treated as if they were constitutive of actual objects, these concepts give rise to a series of metaphysical antinomies, whose solution Kant claims to have discovered.

In a similar way, both the idea of the unconscious as totality (understood in terms of the category of community rather than substance) and the idea of the subject as its "dynamical" corollary are regulative concepts which guide metapsychology. Treated as if they were constitutive of actual objects, they too would give rise to a series of antinomies.

Each of the Kantian antinomies corresponds to a particular principle of the understanding. The overarching concept guiding reason in the antinomies is the category of causality. Each pair of antinomies reflects a particular moment of the judgment that the category of causality can be extended beyond the limits of possible experience.

In chapter 4, I argued that Kant's principles of the understanding represent perverse schemata that map obsessional neurotic symptoms on to hysterical neurotic symptoms. If we think of the schemata as structures of experience, they can be imagined to have a kind of stability that would correspond to the strength of the "sense of reality" posited by the obsessional ego (the "I think" of the understanding). Strictly speaking, this sense of reality is structured like a fantasy—a fact which does not entirely escape the Kantian subject of apperception, who "knows" that its version of reality ultimately counts merely as appearance. The movement from the pleasure principle to the reality principle can be characterized, I have suggested, in terms of a shift from a hallucinatory free play of imagination to the subordination of imagination to the understanding—with results whose stability can be more or less precarious. Freud calls attention to the provisional character of the work of understanding when he suggests that "Thinking . . . is essentially an experimental way of acting" (*SE* XII, 221).

This provisional, experimental character of thought is obscured by the understanding's strong censorship of the imagination. Nonetheless, the sense of reality maintained by this censorship is fragile. On the one hand, the imagination threatens to overstep the bounds of sense, violating the principles which limit thought to what counts as a possible object of experience. On the other hand, and in order to counter this tendency, the understanding threatens to extend its principles so as to eliminate the gap between reality and the "Real" which underlies reality. Either the imagination or the understanding can prompt reason to action here. Kant's apparent strategy is to play the two sides off each other via his critique of the antinomies of reason.

Corresponding to the division of the principles of understanding, there are two sorts of antinomies—mathematical and dynamical. The former give rise to ideas which have no possible legitimate employment. Their objects, accordingly, are classified as mere hallucinations which bespeak a suspension of the reality principle. The dynamical antinomies give rise to ideas that have a possible legitimate employment—but only if the subject imagines a gap separating reality (phenomena) from the Real (noumena). Insofar as the subject takes itself to know the objects given in these latter ideas, it is, Kant suggests, delusional—again signaling a breakdown of the reality principle. However, such delusion, I will argue, arises not in the dynamical theses themselves but in their "regulative" reinvocation after Kant has critiqued the antinomies. The difference between mere illusion at the level of a thesis and full-blown delusion at the level of the "as if knowing" will be strictly maintained.

Insofar as the ideas posited in the theses represent a violation of the reality principle, they can be expected to make conscious the repressed ideas upon which the principles of the understanding rest. Part of the aim of Kant's critique of the antinomies is to prevent the subject from succumbing to these hallucinations. However, the antitheses—especially of the third and fourth antinomies—represent an illegitimate strengthening of the censorship of the understanding. This represents an attempt to eliminate the gap between reality and the Real through an extension of the reality principle. Kant will oppose this reduction by maintaining the possible validity of the theses.

The repressed fantasies of the dynamical principles concerned the idea of Woman and the idea of the phallic mother. At the level of the antinomies, the repressed fantasy of Woman becomes manifest as the conscious idea of a necessarily existing being. In this context, I would invoke Žižek's observation that "Woman" is one of the "names of the father" (Žižek 1995, 24). In a similar way, the fantasy of the phallic mother gives rise to the conscious idea of the phallus. The idea of having the phallus can be equated with Kant's idea of freedom.

The mathematical principles expressed the obsessional interpretation of hysteria and obsessional neurosis proper. When the imagination attempts to go beyond the limits of experience, the easing of the censorship of these principles gives rise to the ideas, respectively, of the cause of hysterical symptoms and the cause of the faculty of judgment itself. In the former case, the subject imagines that it can trace the experience of the hysteric to its simple cause—i.e., the logic of the signifier. In other words, what Kant represents as the simple in the second antinomy could be equated with the indivisibility of the signifier. In the case of obsessional neurosis, the subject could be said to discover that its experience can be explained in terms of the *point de capiton*, or "quilting point," which links signifiers on to objects of experience. The quilting point, in other words, would define both the starting point of experience (the first countable moment in time) and the limits of signification (the boundaries of outer intuition insofar as these are subsumed under the logic of the signifier).

What happens to the schemata of experience when reason, at the prompting of the imagination, seeks to discover their cause? The answer, I suggest, is that these hitherto relatively stable structures begin to disintegrate, giving way to a schizophrenic conflict between the moment of hysterical being and the moment of obsessional thinking.

Freud notes that schizophrenia appears to involve a withdrawal from reality. Yet, like paranoia, it also seems to exhibit an attempt to "cure" itself by reconstructing the lost reality. If we treat these two tendencies as symmetrical opposites, then a dynamic and diachronic picture of schizophrenia emerges whereby first a loss of reality occurs and then an attempt to regain or reconstruct this lost reality takes place. But if we treat the "loss" and "attempt at a cure" as correlative aspects of a single tendency, then a different picture emerges.

Here we have to keep in mind the ambiguous status that the concept of "reality" has in Freud's writings. If the schizophrenic is motivated by a search for the Real behind reality, then this movement can appear both as a turning away from reality and a simultaneous turning toward the Real. If there is a struggle between opposing forces at work, this would reflect a conflict between the imagination and the understanding in their competing attempts to conquer the domain of the Real. The schizophrenic is in effect forced to shift back and forth between a suspending of and an extending of the reality principle—as is exhibited in the logic of the antinomies.

At the level where reason becomes aware of the antinomical character of its reasoning, there arises a schizophrenic logic whereby the subject shifts between its fantasies concerning the Real and its hyperextension of the limits of reality. This shifting reflects a fundamental ambivalence in the attitude of the narcissistic subject toward the world. This ambivalence arises from the dynamical play of imagination, which posits objects of cognition without submitting them to the reality-testing of the understanding. Insofar as the subject appears to itself qua narcissistic soul in relation to possible (rather than actual) objects of experience, it is cut off from itself qua unconscious in relation to impossible objects of experience. This split—the split between the "I" and the "it"—reappears in the antinomies, where the subject goes back and forth between positing a possible object which turns out to be impossible (in the antitheses), and positing the impossibility of an object which turns out to be possible (in the theses). It is for this reason that Kant presents the claims of the antinomies in the form of *reductio ad absurdum* arguments.

In the previous chapter, I noted the opposition that arises from the conflict between the second and third paralogisms of the unconscious: the "choice" between two distinct ways in which the subject might represent itself qua barred subject. As already indicated, Žižek suggests that this choice between thinking and being can be used to explain Lacan's theory of the difference between masculine and feminine subject positions:

> —The "masculine" *cogito* chooses being, the "I am," yet what it gets is being which is merely thought, not real being (*cogito "ergo sum,"* I think "therefore I am," as Lacan writes it), i.e., it gets the fantasy-being, the being of a "person," the being in "reality" whose frame is structured by fantasy.
>
> —The "feminine" *cogito* chooses thought, the pure "I think," yet what it gets is thought bereft of any further predicates, thought which coincides with pure being, or, more precisely, the hyperbolic point which is neither thought nor being. (Žižek 1993, 61–62)

In order to appreciate the dialectical logic at work here, we have to notice that each of the *cogitos* gets the opposite of what it purportedly aims at.

If we write the Cartesian masculine *cogito* as "I think, therefore I am," the ostensible goal of the subject is to establish its own existence—i.e., to attain the "I am." But, precisely in the same way that the drive circles around and misses its supposedly intended object, so here the "I think" in effect sends out an arrow that circles around the "I am," so that instead of its being attained, it remains something merely thought. It is in this sense that the masculine *cogito* manifests itself as an "I think, therefore *it*—i.e., that which I seek but am not—is." The alternative strategy, associated with the feminine *cogito,* is to start from the "I am" in order to "choose" thought. This can be expressed in the formula, "I am, therefore I think." But again, the ostensible object is missed, and so we get "I am, therefore it—i.e., that which I seek but am not—thinks."

Žižek and Copjec suggest that the logic of Lacan's formulae of sexuation parallels that of Kant's antinomies. On their reading, the opposition between the two cogitos reflects not the thesis and antithesis of a given antinomy, but the difference between Kant's mathematical antinomies, on the one hand, and the dynamical antinomies, on the other. Žižek argues as follows:

> Lacan endeavored to formalize sexual difference qua discursive fact by means of his "formulae of sexuation," in which on the "masculine" side the universal function (Vx·Fx: all x are submitted to the function F) implies the existence of an exception (Ex·notFx: there is at least one x which is exempted from the function F), whereas on the feminine side of a particular negation (notVx·Fx: not-all x are submitted to the function F) implies that there is no exception (notEx·notFx: there is no x which could be exempted from the function F). . . . What we have to be attentive to apropos of these formulae of sexuation is that they are structured like antinomies in the Kantian sense. . . .
>
> The first two ("mathematical") antinomies are "feminine" and reproduce the paradoxes of the Lacanian logic of "not-all"; whereas the last two ("dynamical") antinomies are "masculine" and reproduce the paradoxes of universality constituted through exception. (Žižek 1993, 56–57)

Leaving aside, for the moment, the question of why the formulae of sexuation should be structured this way, we can see why Žižek would associate them with the Kantian antinomies as he does. On Lacan's view, the formulae of sexuation are characterized by complementary forms of antinomical reasoning. At face value, these formulae seem to express contradictions. For instance, how could we possibly say that the formula Vx·Fx implies the exception, Ex·notFx? Yet, when we look at Kant's third and fourth antinomies, we find precisely this kind of reasoning at work. For it is precisely the recognition of the fact that all phenomenal events are caused which is immediately supplemented by the positing of an uncaused event. Similarly, it is reason's recognition that all beings are contingent that is immediately supplemented by the claim that there must exist a necessary being. Looking at the first two antinomies, we do indeed find that their theses can be read as implying notVx·Fx, and their antitheses as having the form notEx·notFx. For example, part of the thesis of the first antinomy can be read as saying that not all events are preceded by another event in time; the antithesis can be taken to say that there does not exist any event which is not preceded by another event in time.

How, then, is the split between these pairs of antinomies supposed to be related to the choice between the masculine and feminine *cogitos*? Although it "chooses" being, the masculine subject gets a mere fantasy-being; the recognition of itself as "Real" eludes it. For Žižek, this is precisely the position of the subject of the dynamical antinomies—especially the third antinomy—for whom the existence of the phenomenal world is a mere fantasy-frame which implies a possible noumenal reality for the subject beyond it. Similarly, while the feminine subject "chooses" thought, what it gets is a world which has no reality whatsoever. We see this evidenced, for Žižek, in Kant's argument that both the theses and the antitheses of the first two antinomies are false.

Like Žižek, Copjec takes the "choice" between mathematical and dynamical antinomies to represent the alternatives of feminine and masculine subject positions. She goes on to argue that the structural similarity between Kant's antinomies and Lacan's formulae of sexuation demonstrates the difference between affirming the bisexuality of the subject and claiming that all gender distinctions ultimately collapse. Her argument seems to be roughly as follows. Both masculine and feminine standpoints are "bisexual" in that each affirms a pair of "masculine" and "feminine" claims (either a masculine thesis and a feminine antithesis or a feminine thesis and a masculine antithesis). However, the type of bisexuality represented in each case is different, so that there remains a difference between masculine and feminine bisexuality. Accordingly, Copjec suggests, psychoanalysis appropriately deconstructs the distinction between pure femininity or pure masculinity, but it does not inappropriately deconstruct the difference between masculine bisexuality and feminine bisexuality:

> So you see, there's no use trying to teach psychoanalysis about undecidability, about the way sexual signifiers refuse to sort themselves

> out into two separate classes. It's no use preaching deconstruction to psychoanalysis because it already knows all about it. Bisexuality was long a psychoanalytic concept before it was ever a deconstructionist one. *But the difference between deconstruction and psychoanalysis is that the latter does not confuse the fact of bisexuality—that is, the fact that male and female signifiers cannot be distinguished absolutely—with a denial of sexual difference.* (Copjec 1995, 216; her italics)

Because the two possible resolutions of the *cogito*'s supposedly forced "choice" between being and thinking structurally imply each other, the taking-up of a gender position will involve the repressing of the other possibility. This is why the bisexual *cogito*—or what Freud calls "the constitutional bisexuality of each individual" (*SE* XIX, 31)—remains something repressed. The fact of bisexuality in masculine-identified or feminine-identified subjects explains why each of the dominant claims of the formulae of sexuation should seem to entail a claim which contradicts it. In effect, the formulae of sexuation are structured like antinomies with manifest theses and repressed antitheses.

However, by insisting nonetheless on the "choice" between masculine and feminine subjectivities, Žižek and Copjec seem to foreclose the schizophrenic logic which informs the impossible balancing act of maintaining bisexuality without gender identification. In fact, we might wonder if it is precisely the insistence that the subject "solve" the "meta-antinomy" that opposes the logical forms of the mathematical and dynamical antinomies which threatens to push the subject out of its schizophrenic dilemma into a paranoid insistence on gender identification. It is, of course, the Oedipal conflict which represents the imperative that the subject find just such a solution. To this extent, Deleuze and Guattari might be right to oppose the logic of the schizo to the Oedipal insistence on gender identification. The question is whether Žižek and Copjec reiterate an Oedipal norm when they claim that it is impossible to deconstruct the opposition between masculine and feminine subject positions. By insisting on the necessity of gender "choice," they seem almost to take the position of Ernest Jones, whom Lacan criticizes for claiming to "win the day with the Biblical 'God created them man and woman'" (Lacan 1977, 283). Unlike Jones, of course, neither treats gender identity as a natural phenomenon. In fact, Copjec goes so far as to claim that both masculinity and femininity are mere charades: "All pretentions of masculinity are, then, sheer imposture; just as every display of femininity is sheer masquerade" (Copjec, 234). Nonetheless, she insists that femininity is the proper masquerade of women and masculinity the proper imposture of men, which leads to formulations such as the following:

> Through his desubstantialization of sex, Lacan has allowed us to perceive the fraudulence at the heart of every claim to positive sexual identity. And he has done this equally for men and for women. Which is not to say that he has treated them symmetrically or conceived them as complements of each other. (Copjec, 234)

Against this insistence on strict sexual markers, it is worth recalling that Freud's bisexuality thesis purports to demonstrate the impossibility of demarcating rigidly distinct gender positions:

> The reactions of human individuals of both sexes are of course made up of masculine and feminine traits. . . . All human individuals, as a result of their bisexual disposition and cross-inheritance, combine in themselves both masculine and feminine characteristics, so that pure masculinity and femininity remain theoretical constructions of uncertain content. (*SE* XIX, 255, 258)

Rather than read the difference between the mathematical and dynamical antinomies in terms of Lacan's formulae of sexuation, I suggest that we think of the antinomies as manifesting a conflict between a feminine thesis and a masculine antithesis. More specifically, the feminine theses would represent imaginary ideas arising from a suspension of the subsumption of hysterical symptoms under obsessional laws. As such, the theses would represent "spatial" possibilities even where what is at issue is, as in the first antinomy, the question concerning a first moment in time. If we go back to the idea of spatiality as the site of the mirror stage, the question about a first moment in time would be, precisely, the question concerning the origin of the obsessional subject's shift to temporality. In other words, just as at the level of the principles we found obsessional theorizing of the hysterical, so at the level of the theses of the antinomies we find hysterical speculation on the cause of obsessional symptoms.

Thus, the ideas of a first moment in time, of an outer limit of space, of a simple element of time and space, of freedom, and of necessary being—all would represent imaginary fantasies the possibilities of which are foreclosed in obsessional neurosis. Is it not striking to notice that each of these ideas has become an explicit or implicit topic in the work of feminist metapsychologists such as Irigaray?

It is possible to apply Lacan's formulae of sexuation to the antinomies in the way I have described them. Each of the theses could be said to oppose a masculine claim to universality (governed by a particular principle of the understanding) to an exclusion which is, precisely, the manifest idea posited in the theses. By contrast, each of the antitheses could be said to oppose the feminine exclusion with a reassertion of the claim of universality. So, for example, in the first antinomy, the feminine thesis could be read as saying that although in the symbolic order there does not exist a single moment or place that is not governed by the reality principle, nonetheless not all moments and places are subject to this law. Similarly, the antithesis could be read as saying that, even though the imagination posits an exception to the reality principle, nonetheless all moments and places are subject to this law. The same approach could be carried out with respect to each of the other antinomies as well—both mathematical and dynamical.

The crucial question, it seems to me, is whether what I have characterized as a schizophrenic oscillation between gender possibilities should be treated as a position to be normalized (thereby tending inevitably, I will argue, toward paranoiac gender identifications), or whether it represents an aporia the maintenance of which might present an alternative response to the Oedipal imperative. (I hasten to note that this is not to "romanticize" that which is diagnosed as "clinical" schizophrenia, as some readers of Deleuze and Guattari have charged. Here I would stress the distinction between the schizophrenic as "conceptual persona" and the schizophrenic as "psychosocial type" (Deleuze and Guattari 1994, 122). However, I think it can also be shown that the way in which Freud characterizes schizophrenia (or "paraphrenia") is in keeping with the description that I am proposing here.

The schizophrenic is essentially a subject who notices and refuses to resolve antinomies. Freud calls attention to this phenomenon by characterizing the schizophrenic as someone who posits a split between ideas of words and ideas of things (*SE* XIV, 201). Unlike the "normal" subject, whose normality consists in his or her ability to make judgments about objects, the schizophrenic's cognitive drive is interrupted by a suspension of the schemata that link words and things. As a result of this breakdown in cognitive functioning, the schizophrenic recognizes that what counts as reality for normal subjects rests on a repressed fantasmatic support. Thus, it is not surprising to find the schizophrenic engage in metapsychological speculation. Freud sees in the schizophrenic's cathexes of ideas of words an attempt at a "cure"—by which he means a regaining of the normal parameters of reality. What if, instead, we were to read the schizophrenic's attempt at a cure as an effort to free itself from these very parameters?

Precisely herein would lie the double bind. On the one hand, the schizophrenic will construct a set of metapsychological concepts designed to explain the logic of the cognitive drive. But this set of concepts would purport to constitute another ontology, which the schizophrenic expressly rejects. Thus, on the other hand, the schizophrenic will negate each of its explanations of the nature of the cognitive drive. This perpetual restlessness gives rise to what appears to be the endless play of metonymy and metaphor in the language of schizophrenics. The schizophrenic goes back and forth between theses and antitheses of antinomies without ever resolving them. In this sense, the schizophrenic is a kind of hypercritical metapsychologist, wary of obsessional solutions to problems of gender.

Schizophrenia marks the breakdown of masculine perversion precisely insofar as it severs the link between the ideas of words and the ideas of things. In effect, this marks a refusal to limit the imagination to the rules provided for it by the understanding. Put otherwise, schizophrenia is the result of a suspension of schemata. It is this suspension of the schematism which allows the repressed fantasies to become conscious, and which prompts the understanding to turn away from "reality" and toward the psychic apparatus itself—seeking now not true descriptions of objects of experience but true descriptions of the functioning of the psychic apparatus itself. Herein lies the tendency of the understanding to found a constitutive metapsychology. It provides this through a kind of reconstruction of the logic of the schematism—not as a Kantian deduction of principles, but as a Lacanian articulation of discourses. The schizophrenic subject, however, now suspends these discursive schemata as well. Yet, the positing of these discursive schemata were precisely what allowed it to suspend the Kantian schemata in the first place. Precisely here the schizophrenic finds itself bouncing back and forth between the affirmation and negation of its metapsychological explanations.

It is in this way that metapsychology gives rise to its own antinomies, which concern the following four ideas (taken in reverse order from the order in which Kant presents them): the idea of the Other, the idea of the phallus, the idea of the signifier, and the idea of the quilting point. In its attempt to explain structures of experience by way of these concepts, metapsychology proposes four theses, each of which corresponds to an extension of its critique of a particular principle of the understanding. In its regulative antithetic, it opposes to these theses four corresponding antitheses:

First Conflict of the Metapsychological Ideas

| *Thesis* | *Antithesis* |
|---|---|
| The subject exists in relation to the Other. | The subject does not exist in relation to the Other. |

Second Conflict of the Metapsychological Ideas

| *Thesis* | *Antithesis* |
|---|---|
| The subject exists in relation to the phallus. | The subject does not exist in relation to the phallus. |

Third Conflict of the Metapsychological Ideas

| *Thesis* | *Antithesis* |
|---|---|
| The unconscious is composed of signifiers. | The unconscious is not composed of signifiers. |

Fourth Conflict of the Metapsychological Ideas

| *Thesis* | *Antithesis* |
|---|---|
| The unconscious is constituted by a quilting point. | The unconscious is not constituted by a quilting point. |

What we find exhibited in these antinomies is, so to speak, an "internal conflict" that results from metapsychology's attempt to produce an ontology. The question is whether or not these conflicts can or should be "solved"—and if so, how. Obviously, one way would be to opt for both/and solutions; a second approach would be to opt for neither/nor solutions; and a third approach would be to split the difference and distinguish between two feminine antinomies and two masculine antinomies. But here the question arises as to whether any of these approaches would interrupt the demand of Oedipal normalization. If, moreover, we connect the demand of Oedipal normalization with the governing of the reality principle, it is likely that the insistence on gender identification will itself reflect a masculine injunction. Consider in this connection Freud's observation that the unconscious knows no such thing as contradiction, and therefore has no need to solve antinomies. On the account I am developing, it would be not the imagination but the understanding that would insist on "resolving" the antinomies in some way.

Here we might suspect that there is a difference between the affirmative and negative judgments, as judgments which support the reality principle, and the infinite judgment as that which specifies the limit beyond which the understanding cannot go. If so, then perhaps the schizophrenic can refuse the alternative of affirmative and negative judgments which are presented in antinomies in general by opting for a strategy of infinite judging. I take it that this would yield the following "deconstructive" solutions—or, perhaps better put, deconstructions (i.e., "nonsolutions") of the antinomies:

1. The subject exists in relation to the non-Other.
2. The subject exists in relation to the nonphallus.

3. The unconscious is composed of nonsignifiers.
4. The unconscious is constituted by a nonquilting point.

This would give us a way of articulating the transition from constitutive to regulative metapsychology. Strictly speaking, metapsychology posits its "ontology" only at the level of the signifier and denies the existence of any objects that would correspond to—i.e., be signified by—these signifiers (though obviously the difficulty of this procedure is evidenced in the exception thereby made of the idea of the signifier itself). In this sense, Lacanian theory can be defended on the grounds that it too—i.e., like deconstruction—rejects the claims of ontology. Ultimately, however, this point can be maintained only through an anasemia of the fundamental concepts of metapsychology itself.

A deconstructive approach would also allow us to take account of the irreducible difference between cognitive gender possibilities without requiring obsessional solutions. Even if it turned out that the subject is always split between temporal thinking and spatial being, it need not adopt a gender position that already reflects the submission of spatial being to temporal laws. This suggests not only that spatiality would have to be reconceived, but that temporality would have to be reconceived as well. This point has been made by Irigaray: "The transition to a new age requires a change in our perception and conception of *space-time*" (Irigaray 1993, 7).

What drives the Kantian system is, precisely, the drive which submits both space and time to law: "The subject, the master of time, becomes the axis of the world's ordering, with its something beyond the moment and eternity: God" (Irigaray 1993, 7). Against the law of the Kantian father, the schizophrenic attempts to sidestep this law, thereby opening up the possibility of alternative gender identifications. Might this also mark the difference between acting as if one believed one were gendered and acting as if one knew oneself to be gendered?

One crucial question that still has to be raised concerns the aetiology of what Freud diagnoses as paranoia. In his reading of the memoirs of Schreber, Freud suggests that paranoia results from the refusal of a subject (usually a subject that identifies itself as male) to recognize its own bisexuality: "What lies at the core of the conflict in cases of paranoia among males is a homosexual wishful phantasy of *loving a man*" (*SE* XII, 62). Leaving aside for the moment some complications that Lacan introduces into this framework, Freud suggests that it is the masculine repression of a homosexual fantasy that leads to the metaphysical delusions of paranoia. The question, then, would be this. Is the paranoiac refusal of bisexuality to be correlated, as would follow from Copjec and Žižek's account, with a man's refusal to recognize that he too necessarily affirms dynamical antitheses? Or is it to be correlated with the refusal to recognize that the difference between masculine bisexuality and feminine bisexuality ultimately breaks down as well? Might it turn out that only a schizophrenic refusal of the either/or logic of gender opposition could avoid a paranoid insistence on the presence or absence of the Other?

7

# Ideals of Paranoia

> In Schreber's system the two principal elements of his delusions (his transformation into a woman and his favoured relation to God) are linked in his assumption of a feminine attitude towards God. It will be an unavoidable part of our task to show that there is an essential *genetic* relation between these two elements. Otherwise our attempts at elucidating Schreber's delusions will leave us in the absurd position described in Kant's famous simile in the *Critique of Pure Reason*—we shall be like a man holding a sieve under a he-goat while some one else milks it.
> —Freud *SE* XII, 34

> It remains for the future to decide whether there is more delusion in my theory than I should like to admit, or whether there is more truth in Schreber's delusion than other people are as yet prepared to believe.
> —Freud *SE* XII, 79

If schizophrenia results from the struggle between the imagination and the understanding, paranoia can be said to result when the understanding wins. More precisely, paranoia arises when the principles of the understanding are extended beyond empirical reality to the order of the Real—thereby impelling the imagination to schematize where no empirical objects appear whatsoever. In this sense, the paranoiac is an obsessional neurotic with a vengeance.

Earlier I suggested that in the antinomies we find the imagination positing theses which the understanding rejects in the antitheses. Not to be overlooked, however, is the fact that the antitheses also go beyond the limits of possible experience. When Kant solves the mathematical antinomies by treating both the thesis and the antithesis as false, he in effect cancels their effect, returning reason to the constraints of reality posited by the principles themselves. But when he solves the dynamical antinomies by allowing that both might be true, he allows both the imagination and the understanding to wander into the Real.

The idea of the fourth antinomy, the idea of a necessary being—or, in the fourth metapsychological antinomy, the idea of the Other—is, on my account, an idea posited by the imagination. Now, when Kant turns from the antinomies to the ideal of reason, he invokes the idea of an actual being (*ens realissimum*) that possesses complete reality (*omnitudo realitatis*). By this he means the traditional idea of God. Of course, in keeping with a classical definition of God as necessary being, it would seem that the idea of the fourth antinomy could also be taken as an idea of God. This would suggest that Kant simply imports the idea of the fourth antinomy in his treatment of the ideal of pure reason. Yet, this is not quite the case. By itself, Kant maintains, the idea of a necessary being is simply the idea of *some* necessary being, and as such remains an insufficiently determinate concept to qualify as the idea of God (A586/B614). Reason proposes the concept of an *ens realissimum* as a way of giving content to the mere idea of a necessary being:

> The concept of an *ens realissimum* is therefore, of all concepts of possible things, that which best squares with [*schikken*] the concept of an unconditionally necessary being; and though it may not be completely adequate to it, we have no choice in the matter, but find ourselves constrained to hold it [*so haben wir doch keine Wahl, sondern sehen uns genötigt, uns an ihn zu halten*]. . . . Such, then, is the natural procedure of human reason. It begins by persuading itself of the existence [*Dasein*] of *some* necessary being. This being it apprehends as having an existence [*Existenz*] that is unconditioned. It then looks around for the concept of that which is independent of any condition, and finds it in that which is itself the sufficient condition of all else, that is, in that which contains all reality. (A586–87/B614–15)

Why is this transition from the idea of a necessary being to the idea of an *ens realissimum* so crucial, and why does a gap remain separating the two concepts from each other? I suggest the following interpretation. The idea of a necessary being is an idea posited by the imagination and opposed by the censorship. However, once the understanding realizes that the gap between reality and the Real—the gap between phenomena and noumena—prevents it from censoring the imagination here, it has reason "bind" this idea by bringing it under a determinate concept (reason's idea of an *ens realissimum*). In other words, at the level of the antinomies, the ideas of the dynamical theses had been indeterminate. The fact that the imagination allows for different possible determinations of its ideas parallels the fact that, according to Freud, cathexes in the unconscious remain mobile (*SE* XII, 221). In being bound by reason, the ideas become determinate representations of the Real. In this way, the censorship is reinstated at a higher level, as reason is now given the task of specifying regulative rules for the imagination to follow. More precisely, to use the language that Kant invokes in the third Critique, the imagination is constrained by reason to construct not schemata but *symbols* (Kant 1987, 225–26).

To clarify the topographical point once again, the idea of a necessary being originates in the imagination; the idea of an *ens realissimum* originates in the understanding. In saying this, of course, I am treating the Kantian distinction between the understanding and reason fairly loosely. But this seems justified by the fact that the split between the understanding and reason can be likened to the split between the ego and the ego ideal. Freud explicitly leaves open the question of how "to localize the ego ideal," specifically with respect to the issue of whether the ego ideal should be treated as a part of the ego or not (*SE* XIX, 36–37). In a similarly ambiguous way, Kant characterizes reason as exerting its force on the understanding, at times supposedly compelling it to overstep the boundaries of experience and at times preventing it from doing so. In this last respect, we can see how ambiguous the agency of reason might be: Is it censoring the imagination or is it censoring the understanding? Just as the superego is said to incorporate elements of both the id and the ego, so on the account I am giving reason might be said to incorporate elements of both the imagination and the understanding. In this sense, the faculty of reason—particularly in its critical employment—might not be just an agency of censorship, but would in certain respects represent a kind of compromise formation.

The fundamental difference between the ideas of reason and the categories of the understanding is that the latter are applicable to reality, the former to the Real. Lacking the mediation of sensibility, the idea of the *ens realissimum* is treated as if it were an actual object grasped through intellectual intuition. It is for this reason that Kant calls it an *ideal* rather than merely an idea:

> It is therefore a transcendental *ideal* which serves as basis for the complete determination that necessarily belongs to all that exists. This ideal is the supreme and complete material condition of the possibility of all that exists—the condition to which all thought of objects, so far as their content is concerned, has to be traced back. It is also the only true ideal of which human reason is capable. (A576/B604)

However, this being cannot be known through intellectual intuition, which according to Kant we do not possess. Hence "all our cognition of God is merely symbolic" (Kant 1987, 228).

If the idea of a necessary being already corresponds to Lacan's idea of the Other, what would be the Lacanian parallel to the ideal of reason? Here it is important to keep in mind that for Lacan, the Other is the barred Other, which indicates both that the Other exists only as nonexisting and that it has no determinate content. As such, the barred Other can be likened to the idea of a necessary being insofar as the latter is an idea of the imagination. By contrast, the ideal of reason—which, qua ideal, is presumed to exist and which, qua *ens realissimum*, is presumed to have determinate content—would correspond to what Lacan calls the *unbarred* Other. It is this, above all, that warrants the association between the Kantian ideal and the subject position assumed in paranoia.

It is important to realize, in other words, that Lacan is essentially a critic of Kant on this point, for it would be a mistake to read the thesis of the fourth metapsychological antinomy—or, more precisely, the metapsychological solution to this fourth antinomy—as positing the Kantian ideal. For similar reasons, it would be a mistake to read the antithesis of the fourth antinomy as sufficiently side-stepping the problematic of the Kantian ideal. As Deleuze points out, the claim that "God is dead" is itself a theological affirmation and for this reason serves merely as a starting point for Nietzsche's more radical critique of the value of truth. In fact, to herald the death of God is simply another way of shifting from the fourth antinomy to the Kantian ideal, for this ideal—as *omnitudo realitatis*—is nothing other than truth itself. Far from displacing the concept of God, the "truth" that God is dead would merely take God's place—or, more precisely, would be God with a new name. This is why Nietzsche has his madman declare that the atheists in the marketplace do not understand the meaning of the death of God. Much as Kant distinguishes between the deist and the theist, noting that while the latter believes in a living God, the former believes in a non-living God (A633/B661), so Nietzsche in effect suggests that the atheist who believes in the death of God is but a deist in disguise.

What this suggests is that either the affirmation (thesis) or negation (antithesis) of the idea of the fourth antinomy can be taken up in the Kantian ideal of reason. Or, more precisely, the ideal of reason might be nothing other than the dialectical *Aufhebung* of the fourth antinomy. That is, perhaps it is precisely by opting for a "both/and" solution that reason manages to "bind" the imaginary cathexis of the thesis to the symbolic anticathexis of the antithesis.

Here I would recall that, according to Žižek and Copjec, the strategy of a "both/and" solution is that of masculine subjectivity. Without giving up my earlier suggestion that the conflict between feminine and masculine positions would manifest themselves in each of the antinomies, here I would agree that Kant "solves" the dynamical antinomies through specifically masculine solutions. This is to be understood in the specific sense that the antitheses subsume the theses, much in the way that the principles of the understanding subsume hysterical symptoms under obsessional symptoms. But if this is so, then to posit the Kantian ideal of reason would be to remain within an essentially masculine paradigm. More precisely, it would be to pass from a merely obsessional masculinity to a paranoiac masculinity—precisely of the sort that Freud detects in Schreber's ideal of a God who demands a state of constant enjoyment.

Here we need to consider the specificity of what in the previous chapter I called metapsychology's possibility of a deconstructive solution to the fourth antinomy—namely, construing the barred Other as the "non-Other." The object of an infinite judgment cannot be "bound" by an anticathexis of the understanding. That is, by not subsuming the free play of imagination under any determinate concepts of the understanding, the deconstructive infinite judgment interrupts the shift from the schizophrenic double-bind to the paranoiac insistence on a masculine Real. The idea of the non-Other would maintain the gap between reality and the Real with an imaginary marker that could not be transformed into a symbol of reason. The deconstructive conception of the non-Other would invoke the Lacanian barred Other, but in such a way as to allow for an open-ended "as if believing" rather than a law that demands "as if knowing." In this way, a deconstructive reading of metapsychology would prevent the foreclosure of the imagination.

Lacan, of course, makes the concept of foreclosure (*Verwerfung*) central to his account of the formation of paranoia (Lacan 1977, 200ff.). Whereas the neuroses and perversions can be explained in terms of repression, he claims, the psychoses arise from a foreclosure that entirely eliminates a signifier from the subject's signifying field. What is foreclosed for Schreber is the signifier of the name-of-the-father—the signifying support of the symbolic order. I take it that the symbolic order is equivalent to reality as constituted by the understanding; however, the signifying support of the understanding is provided, precisely, by the imagination. There remains, nonetheless, a topographical ambiguity in Lacan's location of the name-of-the-father, which he situates in the field of the symbolic rather than in the field of the imaginary. On his account, foreclosure introduces a hole in the symbolic order which then produces a corresponding hole in the imaginary order. Interpreted in this way, Schreber's paranoia would seem to spring from a foreclosure of the symbolic order itself.

To the extent that it posits its ideal only through a suspension of the principles of the understanding, it can certainly seem as if reason thereby responds to the hole in the symbolic order which arises when the signifier of the transcendental object is elided. However, this would be to simplify the mechanism in question. If, at the level of the antinomies, a hole is introduced in the symbolic by the imagination, it is not this per se which leads to paranoia. On the contrary, the irruption of this hole simply inaugurates the schizophrenic refusal to let the understanding fill the gap between reality and the Real. In the transition from the antinomies to the ideal, what occurs is a second foreclosure—a foreclosure of the imagination. It is this which is decisive in the constitution of paranoia. Accordingly, we should either say that the name-of-the-father is primarily an imaginary signifier, or we should say that it is not the foreclosure of the name-of-the-father (which perhaps is what gives rise to the antinomies), but the foreclosure of a second signifier (the signifier of the desire of the mother?), which leads to the onset of paranoia. At any rate, whereas the antinomies result from a foreclosure of the support of the symbolic order, paranoia results from a foreclosure of the imaginary order itself. This would help to explain why Lacan thinks that projection cannot be the mechanism of delusion-formation in paranoia, for projection belongs to the work of imagination. For this reason, in his seminar on the psychoses, Lacan distinguishes between "imaginary" and "delusional" projection, suggesting that if projection does play a role in the case of Schreber it is of the delusional sort (Lacan 1993, 145–46). In the essay in which he summarizes the results of this seminar, Lacan discounts the role of projection altogether (Lacan 1977, 188).

The fact that projection can seem both to play a major role in the formation of paranoia and not to play a role in it at all might be explained very simply by thinking of paranoia as one possible resolution to schizophrenia. Projection would take place at the level at which the schizophrenic imagination is positing the theses of its antinomies. Paranoia would result when the understanding forecloses the work of imagination and puts its concepts in the place of the imagination's foreclosed ideas—as in the case of the substitution of the idea of an *ens realissimum* for the idea of a necessary being. This explanation would accord with Freud's recognition of the similarities between schizophrenia and paranoia in its early stages:

> We can understand how a clinical picture such as Schreber's can come about, and merit the name of a paranoid dementia, from the fact that in its production of a wishful phantasy and of hallucinations it shows paraphrenic traits, while in its exciting cause, in its use of the mechanism of projection, and in its outcome it exhibits a paranoid character. (*SE* XII, 77–78)

Freud's picture, however, would need a few minor corrections. Both the production of a wishful fantasy and the mechanism of projection whereby the object of this fantasy is taken to exist in the world would coincide with the positing of the idea of a necessary being. But it is by way of a foreclosure of this mechanism of projection that, paradoxically, the paranoiac ideal of reason appears in the hole that has been left by the foreclosed projection.

All of this, of course, bears on the question of what to make of the relationship between paranoia and gender. Freud tentatively interprets Schreber's delusions as resulting from the projection of a homosexual fantasy:

> The exciting cause of his illness, then, was an outburst of homosexual libido; the object of this libido was probably from the very first his doctor, Flechig; and his struggles against the libidinal impulse produced the conflict which gave rise to the symptoms. (*SE* XII, 43)

Following Ida Macalpine, on the other hand, Lacan argues that the appeal to a repressed homosexual tendency is insufficient for explaining Schreber's symptoms. Along similar lines, others have wondered why a repressed homosexual tendency should lead to symptoms of paranoia in some cases but not in others. Further questions concern the difference between paranoia in men and paranoia in women. Is there such a thing as feminine paranoia? If so, would a paranoiac feminine identity entail a foreclosure of the understanding, parallel to the masculine foreclosure of the imagination? Finally, can gender identification occur otherwise than through a mechanism of paranoia?

If we take the split between being and thinking to reflect the difference between space and time, then the "choice" between hysterical and obsessional symptoms would mark the split between possible gender identifications at the level of the neuroses. At that level, as I suggested, subjects would generally be more or less hysterical, more or less obsessional. At the level of the antinomies, however, the split now becomes an "all or nothing" set of alternatives: that is, the subject must elect either to identify itself as completely masculine or as completely feminine. However, this "choice" would seem to represent a Lacanian "vel"—i.e., an "or" that really allows for no choice at all: what Lacan calls "the *vel* of alienation" (Lacan 1978, 211). Just as in the case of the illusory choice "Your money or your life!" so the supposed choice between "Your feminine imagination or your masculine understanding!" allows for only one possible choice—the supposed "both/and" solution that is the choice of pure masculinity.

However, the schizophrenic refuses this false set of alternatives, hovering between the feminine and the masculine. And the deconstructive solution to these antinomies perhaps allows for a way of maintaining this schizophrenic refusal, without requiring that it either lapse back into "normal" obsessional neurosis or leap into "abnormal" paranoia.

The foreclosure of the imagination which precipitates the transition from schizophrenia to paranoia would thus represent a "collapsing" of the sexually wavering schizophrenic *cogito* into a paranoiac masculine *cogito*. However, unlike the narcissistic *cogito*, whose masculine "I think" remains cut off from its "I am," the paranoiac *cogito* does not merely repress but forecloses the feminine *cogito*. This elision of the feminine "I am" marks a hole which the paranoiac *cogito* then seeks to fill. To see how this process works in Kant, we would need to look at the transition from the idea of the third antinomy—the indeterminate idea of freedom—to the appropriation/foreclosure/substitution of the determinate idea of autonomy which reason introduces. Understood in this way, the subject's identification of itself as autonomous would coincide with the essentially masculine fantasy of taking up the position of Woman. Specifically, Schreber's fantasy of giving birth would coincide with the Kantian fantasy of being an autonomous initiator of causal chains.

Clearly there is a reciprocity between Schreber's idea of the God who calls him a whore and his idea of himself as never living up to the demand to become a woman. Schreber's failure to become a woman—his failure even to form the delusional belief that he had become a woman—might seem to bespeak the impossibility of a masculine subject's assuming the position of a feminine subject simultaneously. Strictly speaking, however, Schreber's failure might be better understood as the impossibility of taking up the position of the foreclosed feminine *cogito*. Here it is important to keep in mind the difference between the schizophrenic—who might very well attempt to adopt both masculine and feminine positions by refusing the work of repression—and the paranoiac, who gives himself the impossible task of taking up a foreclosed position.

It is important, I think, to stress the strict homology between Schreber's relationship to God and the way in which Kant represents the relationship between the autonomous will and God. Like Schreber, the autonomous will must respond to incomplete sentences (the "You must . . ." of the categorical imperative) which have their ultimate source in God. Like Schreber, who never lives up to the demand to become a woman, so Kant's pathological human subject may never live up to the demand to assume the position of autonomous will. For this reason, Kant calls humanity "radically evil" (Kant 1960, 28), an epithet that more or less specifies the rational content of the famous "*Luder!*" which Schreber's

God hurls at him. There is, finally, a clear parallel between Kant's description of the feeling of the sublime and the experience of *jouissance* which Lacan ascribes to Schreber. We experience the sublime whenever our imagination fails to symbolize an idea of reason; according to Kant we first feel humiliation because of this inadequacy but then pleasure because of the superiority of our reason. This dynamic is similar to the way in which Schreber feels both pain and pleasure in his failed attempt to assume the position of Woman. As Micheline Enriquez points out:

> The paranoiac doesn't repeat much, at least in the classical sense of the term. He invests, creates and recreates, he interprets while leaning upon *fixation*—the recording in the purely visual sense of the term, and its corollary, blindness, *so as to graft sense upon non-sense, or to represent the unrepresentable.* (Enriquez 1988, 111; her italics)

Although Enriquez refers neither to Kant nor to the idea of the sublime, it is clear that this is what is at issue here. For the experience of sublimity arises, for Kant, precisely through the attempt to represent the unrepresentable.

Kant, of course, associates a sense of the sublime with men and a sense of the beautiful with women—though he allows that all subjects can have both experiences (Kant 1991, 76–78). In keeping with the reading of Schreber as having foreclosed the feminine, it is not surprising to find Kant associating the sublime with masculinity. For analogous reasons, it might make sense, as Kant suggests, to associate a sense of the beautiful with the feminine. We experience the beautiful when there is a breakdown in the understanding's ability to subsume an object of intuition under a determinate concept. This breakdown could be said to allow the feminine theses of the antinomies to deploy their indeterminate ideas. Possibly the question concerning the bisexual *cogito* can be raised as the question of whether it is possible to experience sublime beauty and/or beautiful sublimity.

But perhaps this is the wrong way to frame the problem. The experience of the sublime is possible, we might say, only on the assumption of a foreclosure of the imagination—indeed, it occurs precisely *as* the experience of this foreclosure. On the other hand, the experience of the beautiful involves not a foreclosure of the understanding but simply a suspension of its principles. The two are by no means equivalent. Were the work of understanding foreclosed entirely, the imagination would give rise to no cognitions whatsoever. Any pleasure resulting from the experience would count, in Kant's terminology, as an experience of charm (*Reiz*) rather than of the beautiful. In the experience of the beautiful, by contrast, the understanding works overtime, because it continuously proposes concepts none of which proves to be adequate to the object to which they are applied. In order for this process to take place, there must be a suspension of the principles that would otherwise lead to finished determinate judgments. This suspension represents not a foreclosure of the understanding but simply an undoing of the repression of the imagination.

Thus, we might say that it is the experiences of the charming and the sublime that represent opposed foreclosures which could be characterized in gendered terms. It is noteworthy that much of what Kant associates with the feminine appreciation of beauty in his early "Observations on the Feeling of the Beautiful and the Sublime" essay falls under the heading of what in the third Critique he will call the merely charming. In the experience of the beautiful in the strict sense, we find that restless "free play of the faculties" which Kant attempts to submit to rules. Here I deliberately leave aside questions of whether Kant's description of the experience of the beautiful is accurate or not. Since his entire exposition remains guided by the logic of the first Critique, he claims that in the experience of the beautiful the imagination "as such" is made subordinate to the understanding "as such"—thereby repeating the obsessional/perverse logic that we found at the level of the principles of the understanding. But suppose we were to read the free play of the faculties as a chaotic interplay, in which no faculty succeeds in imposing a law on the others. This would be a more Deleuzian Kant, and perhaps in this light we could look to the experience of the beautiful to illustrate how a bisexual *cogito* could function as a play of cathexes and anticathexes without giving rise to either the dominance of the obsessional or the foreclosure of the feminine. Significantly, Kant associates the experience of the beautiful with a feeling of cognitive pleasure untainted by any pain. Yet, he resists treating this as the highest form of human feeling. On the contrary—fully in keeping with his Schreberian tendencies—he insists that the experience of the sublime occasions a higher type of pleasure than that which arises in an experience of the beautiful (Kant 1987, 98). Lacan has taught us how to read this suggestion.

Perhaps a type of foreclosure does take place in the experience of the beautiful—a foreclosure of reason. For the free play of faculties concerns, specifically, the faculties of sensibility, imagination, and understanding. The relationships among these faculties in the experience of the beautiful could be represented in terms of Lacan's Borromean knot linking the orders of the Real, the imaginary, and the symbolic. Similarly, we could represent the foreclosure of a particular faculty in terms of the deformed knots that Lacan diagrams.

If I am right, then we should expect to find the experience of the beautiful at work in Lacan's conception of what a therapeutic cure might consist in. In their readings of Lacan, Žižek and Copjec seem to accord pride of place to the experience of the sublime. They invoke Kant's account of radical evil as describing an indestructible feature of the subject's relation to law, and describe the relationship between *jouissance* and the law in strictly Kantian/Schreberian terms. It seems to me that these descriptions of Kantian experience are exactly accurate. The question, however, is whether Kantian experience represents an immutable norm or not. A crucial part of Žižek and Copjec's argument concerns the intractability of the law of the superego. In effect, the law represents the unforeclosable itself. Should we agree with this conclusion? If, as I have argued, reason itself appears only through a foreclosure of imagination, it will itself be structured like a delusion. Assuming it were possible to undo or refuse to undergo such a foreclosure, might this delusion disappear? In this sense, my characterization of the experience of the beautiful as foreclosing reason might be misleading. Strictly speaking, reason is not a separate faculty whose work could be foreclosed; it is simply a delusion constructed by the understanding to fill the gap opened up by the foreclosure of the imagination. Might we not expect, then, that by returning to the possibility of an experience of the beautiful—an experience that perhaps could no longer sustain a rigid dichotomy between inner and outer experience, subject and object—the mirage of the undeconstructible law will disappear?

This question, at any rate, cannot be answered within the horizon of the Kantian project.

# 8

# The Ethics of Psychoanalysis

> What the superego demands has nothing to do with that which we would be right in making the universal rule of our actions; such is the ABC of psychoanalytic truth.
> —Lacan 1992, 310

> Consequently, the reconciliation of the conflicting impulses would involve the removal of this tyranny—that is, the restoration of the right of sensuousness.
> —Marcuse 1974, 190

> In order to make it possible to think through, and live, this difference, we must reconsider the whole problematic of *space* and *time*.
> —Irigaray 1993, 7

At the outset of this book I argued that Kant's critical method was based on an insistence—an insistence on treating limits of experience as synthetic a priori. One might ask: Is that which motivates Kant best represented as an insistence on thinking the synthetic a priori or as a taboo against thinking the analytic a posteriori?

The transcendental philosopher who deploys his cards in the first Critique refuses to play the game of "rationalists (Cartesians) versus empiricists (Lockeans)." Herein might seem to lie the hysterical side of Kant, the side that breaks with the moment of Cartesian mastery represented in both the rationalist and empiricist traditions; it is this that seems to justify Žižek's reading of Kant as adopting the position of the hysteric: "Kant's 'transcendental turn' cuts this link between philosophy and the discourse of the Master: transcendental philosophy 'changes the register' to the discourse of the hysteric" (Žižek 1992, 146). As I have tried to show, however, it is not Kant but Hume—breaking with both Cartesian and Lockean pretensions to mastery—who makes the "quarter turn" to the discourse of the hysteric. Kant's encounter with this discourse leads to a further turn to the discourse of the analyst, from whose subject position Kant will analyze Humean symptoms. This is in keeping, moreover, with an observation Žižek makes elsewhere—namely that the manifest position of the analyst in relation to the barred subject coincides with the Kantian/Sadean formula of perversion (Žižek 1993, 71).

For this reason, in the Kantian philosophy there are not simply three players (rationalists, empiricists, and Kant) but four (rationalists, Lockean empiricists, Hume, and Kant). The hand of the rationalists Kant calls analytic a priori; the hand of the empiricists, synthetic a posteriori. Kant, the dealer, gets the synthetic a priori, and since he takes the bid he gets to call trump. In order to play out his hand, he needs a dummy—the analytic a posteriori—whose cards Kant will play. No one gets to take up the cards of the dummy but the dealer—and only qua dealer, not qua dummy. Thus, this fourth hand never appears as such; it is a "vanishing mediator." By a sleight of hand, Kant will sometimes pretend that Hume is playing the cards of the empiricist, and he will sometimes pretend that he and Hume are playing the same hand.

There is some question as to whether Kant actually read Hume or not: apparently, he knew reviews of Hume's works. (This "missed encounter" would be interesting to compare with Freud's "missed encounter" with Nietzsche.) At any rate, it is clear that Kant conceived of the *Critique* as a point-for-point attempt to refute Humean skepticism. Any parallels between Kant and metapsychology would therefore suggest parallels with Hume as well. The trajectory that links Hume, Kant, Freud, and Lacan might be characterized in terms of Lacan's understanding of the temporality of symptoms:

> The symptom initially appears to us as a trace, which will only ever be a trace, one which will continue not to be understood until the analysis has got quite a long way, and until we have discovered its meaning. In addition, one can say that, just as the *Verdrängung* is only ever a *Nachdrängung*, what we see in the return of the repressed is the effaced signal of something which only takes on its value in the future, through its symbolic realisation, its integration into the history of the subject. Literally, it will only ever be a thing which, at the given moment of its occurrence, *will have been.* (Lacan 1991b, 159)

Humean skepticism, I suggest, is a symptom the significance of which has been progressively constituted in the trajectory that links the works of Hume, Kant, Freud and Lacan. Hume is analyzed by Kant who is analyzed by Freud who is analyzed by Lacan. And, at the end of this process, it turns out that Lacan is suffering from Humean symptoms—or, better put, that the positions of Hume the analysand and Kant the analyst have been reversed.

Hume himself is perhaps best described as the hysteric who speaks of his own desire. The problem with hysterics is not that they don't speak; it's that they don't get listened to. When the dealer takes a card from the dummy's hand, it can seem as if it is the dummy who has played—but the dealer takes the trick. Like Dora, Hume has symptoms which are misdiagnosed if we interpret them from the perspective of the desire of the Kantian analyst. Just as Freud's handling of the case of Dora calls out for analysis, so does Kant's treatment of Hume's questions—particularly as the telos of the Kantian project is to legislate a universal paranoia.

This paranoia, I suggest, has a historical specificity. Teresa Brennan has argued that Lacan is best read not as a transcendental theorist but as a historical theorist of desire (Brennan 1993, 7). Brennan sees Lacan as diagnosing a specific social psychosis that first arises in the modern world—a psychosis that concerns the delusional object which psychoanalysis calls the "ego." Although I agree with a good deal of Brennan's analyses—especially her diagnosis of modernity as an age of paranoia—I suggest that the social psychosis proper to modernity (or, at least, proper to post-Enlightenment modernity) is best understood not in terms of the ego but in terms of the superego.

It seems to me that one could trace the history of modern philosophy from Descartes to Hume to Kant in terms of the movement from paralogisms of narcissism to antinomies of schizophrenia to ideals of paranoia. Descartes, precisely by invoking the ego, would inaugurate the paralogisms of narcissism, which find their fullest development in the empirical idealism of George Berkeley. If Descartes inaugurates an era of the ego, and Hume a brief era (the Scottish Enlightenment?) of the schizo who calls this ego into question, it is Kant who inaugurates the era of the superego. This era remains ours—for despite the successive challenges to Kantianism found in Hegel, Nietzsche, Freud, Lacan, and others, the structure of experience in the age of capital remains, as Brennan shows, that of the paranoiac. My disagreement with Brennan, then, is simply this: where she treats the ego as equivalent to the paranoid subject, I take the ego to be a narcissistic subject who—contrary to the usual critiques of capitalism—is not equivalent to the consumerist subject. It is, rather, the superego that represents the paranoid subject in question.

It is important, in this context, to notice the ways in which Descartes is far less paranoid than Kant. Descartes's silence on moral matters is sometimes taken as a symptom of what is wrong with the Cartesian model of subjectivity. I contend that there is an aspect to this side of Descartes which we might do well to retrieve, for Descartes's silence concerning moral and theological questions arises not from an ethical indifference but from a principled skepticism concerning the ultimate purpose of the world and of human existence. Whatever the problems with its narcissism, the Cartesian subject's skepticism concerning the nature of the good makes it far healthier than what we inherit from Kant—a universal paranoia which takes the absence of a determinate concept of the good as the justification for instituting a ruthless law, thereby transforming narcissistic egos into morally certain despots. Is it not Kantian morality that in this way marks the transition from the mere merchant to the capitalist proper? And lest we read the difference between the two merely as a matter of degree, it is important to notice that the shift from Cartesianism to Kantianism implies a break of some sort—for Kant has to undermine the certainty of the Cartesian subject (hence his critique of the paralogisms) in order to install the authority of the Kantian despot, thereby replacing the temporary reign of a narcissistic ego with the tyranny of the ego ideal.

It is possible that Hume remains vital for us primarily insofar as he represents an alternative to these two positions, a wedge that undermines both. In trying to find our way out of the era of the superego, it is probably necessary to look back to pre-Kantian possibilities in philosophers such as Hume and Spinoza, as well as to analyze the history of the post-Kantian legacy. Hume, of course, is primarily a critic of Cartesianism. I would argue, however, that his chief importance *for us* lies with his resistance to the reign of the superego. This is a side of Hume that appears only in retrospect, after Kant; in keeping with the reverse temporality of the symptom, Hume can in this sense be read as Kant's analyst.

As interrogator of the superego, of course, it is Freud who explicitly takes up the position of Kant's analyst. Perhaps the most crucial text in this regard is *Civilization and Its Discontents,* which can be read as an attempt to rewrite Kant's *Grounding for the Metaphysics of Morals* from a psychoanalytic point of view (much as *Moses and Monotheism* is clearly an attempt to rewrite Nietzsche's *On the Genealogy of Morals*). The parallels between the two works, as Lacan notices, are striking. Kant argues that the pursuit of happiness makes people miserable; Freud argues that not giving up the pleasure principle can only lead to disaster. Kant contrasts the end of happiness with the end of duty; Freud notes the conflict between instinctual demands and the demands of civilization. Kant suggests that if we act from reason we are entitled to believe that we might become happy later; Freud holds out hope that a rational society might also allow for human happiness.

But Freud also rejects crucial tenets of Kant's moral theory. For example, Kant's opposition between actions done because of inclinations and actions done from duty is undermined by Freud's insistence on the libidinal basis of the demands of civilization. In the shift from the pleasure principle to the reality principle—the basis of the Kantian turn from happiness to duty as the proper end of life—Freud shows that the aim of happiness is never abandoned. Unlike Kant, who maintains that the purpose of reason is to promote a good will, Freud traces the function of reason to reality-testing and to the effort at satisfying instinctual demands. For Freud, there simply is no purpose to human life outside the project of eudaimonism, a point that Lacan underscores (Lacan 1992, 13).

But perhaps the most important aim of Freud's work is to attack Kant's attempt to ground morality on the basis of a delusional metaphysical system. The only legitimate justification of religion, Freud maintains, would be its success at promoting happiness; but at this it fails miserably. To pretend, with Kant, that acting from duty might lead to happiness in the next life is merely to admit defeat:

> If the believer finally sees himself obliged to speak of God's "inscrutable decrees," he is admitting that all that is left to him as a last possible consolation and source of pleasure in his suffering is an unconditional submission. And if he is prepared for that, he could probably have spared himself the *détour* he has made. (*SE* XXI, 85)

Against the wish-fulfillment promised by the illusions of religion, Freud offers the guarded pessimism of science. And yet, despite Lacan's suggestion that Freud's appeal to science should be interpreted in ethical terms rather than in ontological terms, Freud thereby ends up confirming the principles of Kant's empirical realism. Although he denies any legitimacy to the ideas of reason (soul, freedom, God), Freud does not leave metaphysics behind; he simply insists on the truth of the antitheses to the Kantian antinomies. Does Freud thereby challenge the delusional belief in an *ens realissimum* or does he simply substitute the God of science for the God of the theologians? As for his refutation of religion, it is based solely on the grounds that religion is an illusion. Obviously, the only grounds for giving up illusion are those given by the reality principle; and it is precisely in the name of the reality principle that Freud treats science not as an illusion but as the revelation of truth.

Freud also rejects the idea that art might sufficiently compensate for instinctual renunciation. Here he cannot accuse art of *Schwärmerei*, as in effect he does religion, for art tries to bring about a compromise between illusion and reality. Hence, Freud can only acknowledge that "Psychoanalysis, unfortunately, has scarcely anything to say about beauty" (*SE* XXI, 83). This does not prevent him from rejecting the idea that art might provide a means for balancing the demands of civilization and the demand for happiness. Freud thereby forecloses the very question that would need to be raised—i.e., the question of whether a "free play of faculties" might present an alternative between the either/or of "pleasure principle versus reality principle." In fact, given his own account of the reality principle as a continuation of the pleasure principle by other means, it is not clear why sublimation couldn't proceed along the lines of an aesthetic impulse. Unfortunately, Freud fails to recognize any distinction between the beautiful and the charming (*Reiz*; translated as *attraction* in the *Standard Edition*), and so he does not conceive of a sense of beauty as that which might result from a harmony of the pleasure and reality principles. Finally, although he acknowledges that an alternative to instinctual renunciation can be found in the experience of love, he rejects the sufficiency of love on the grounds that its supposed demand for exclusivity makes it risk as much as it promises to gain. Having rejected all possibilities for sublimation based on what Kant would call inclination, it is no wonder if Freud should reach a pessimistic conclusion about the possibility of reconciling the demand for happiness with the demands of civilization.

In the end, therefore, Freud seems to strengthen the position of the Kantian superego, and it is here, I take it, that Lacan's question concerning the desire of the analyst becomes especially important. Significantly, Lacan suggests that Freud failed to understand the nature of the hysteric's desire (Lacan 1978, 12). Hence, we should not be surprised to find Freud failing to analyze Kant successfully—not because Kant is a hysteric, but because Freud would have had to take up the position of the hysteric himself in order to analyze Kant. If Lacan can be said to correct the Freudian analysis of Kant (admittedly a complicated question), it would be insofar as he returns to the basic position of Hume's hysterical skepticism. That Lacan can be read as doing just this is what I will now try to suggest.

Let me begin by invoking the following formula, which represents the heart of Lacanian theory:

$$\frac{S}{s}$$

This, of course, is Lacan's algorithm of *signifiance*, to be read as "the signifier over the signified, 'over' corresponding to the bar separating the two stages" (Lacan 1977, 149). The signifier never crosses the bar separating it from the signified. What passes for signification always remains on the order of the signifier itself, in one of two ways. In metonymy, one signifier refers to another solely by virtue of there being some sort of contiguity between them: "It involves substitution for something that has to be named—we are in fact at the level of the name. One thing is named by another that is its container, or its part, or that is connected to it" (Lacan 1993, 221). The other way in which signifiers relate to each other is through metaphor, the substitution of one signifier for another—an identification based on a posited resemblance between the terms being identified.

Metaphor itself is sustained by metonymy:

> The creative spark of the metaphor does not spring from the presentation of two images, that is, of two signifiers equally actualized. It flashes between two signifiers one of which has taken the place of the other in the signifying chain, the occulted signifier remaining present through its (metonymic) connexion with the rest of the chain. (Lacan 1977, 157)

The essential difference between metaphor and metonymy has to do with the bar separating the order of signifiers from the order of signifieds. In metonymy, signifiers merely slide along the bar without ever crossing it. In metaphor, the substitution of one signifier for another conjures an illusion that the bar has been crossed, thereby "indicating that it is in the substitution of signifier for signifier that an effect of signification is produced" (Lacan 1977, 164). The point to be stressed is that "an effect of signification" is not the same as a "successful" crossing of the bar; strictly speaking, no such crossing ever takes place.

In this model, Lacan repeats the basic argument of book 1 of Hume's *Treatise.* For Hume, experience consists solely of impressions and ideas. Let us take the discreteness of simple impressions and ideas to warrant our calling them signifiers. According to Hume, there are three principal ways in which these signifiers become associated with one another. He calls these the principles of association, based on three qualities: resemblance, contiguity in time or place, and cause and effect. There is, however, a significant difference between the first two principles and the last. For, according to Hume, there is never much doubt as to whether two signifiers resemble each other or are contiguous with each other. But there is reason to wonder whether such a thing as cause and effect relations ever take place.

The fact that signifiers which resemble each other should be associated together, thereby allowing for identifications and substitutions, is clearly Hume's principle of metaphor: "our imagination runs easily from one idea to any other that *resembles* it, and . . . this quality alone is to the fancy a sufficient bond and association" (Hume 1978, 11).

That signifiers which are contiguous in time or place should be associated together is Hume's principle of metonymy:

> 'Tis likewise evident, that as the senses, in changing their objects, are necessitated to change them regularly, and take them as they lie *contiguous* to each other, the imagination must by long custom acquire the same method of thinking, and run along the parts of space and time in conceiving its objects. (Hume 1978, 11)

Just as Lacan sees metaphor as involving substitutions which can be reinserted in metonymic chains, so Hume calls attention to the expectation that a resembling signifier will be contiguous with signifiers with which the resembled signifier was contiguous.

If impressions and ideas are signifiers, objects are for Hume what these signifiers purport to signify. In order to pass from the associations of metaphor and metonymy to the idea of the object, however, the imagination must first presume that it can leave the order of the signifier for the order of the signified. Merely to associate two signifiers which resemble each other is to remain at the level of the signifier, but to posit an identity is to imagine that one is dealing with something signified. To show that this is an illusion—i.e., that it is an illusion to think that signifiers ever cross the bar, or that we ever encounter anything other than signifiers—is the primary aim of Hume's book on the understanding. The secondary aim is to explain how this illusion takes place. Hume's answer, translated into Lacanian terms, is to explain how metaphor leads the imagination to posit a falling of the signifier into the order of the signified.

The idea of an object—i.e., the idea of the signified—depends upon the idea of identity. However, the idea of identity is itself dependent on the idea of causality. For we posit an object's being identical to itself even when our perception of it is interrupted, and for Hume this can be explained only on the assumption that we have first considered what the causes might be for the object's being either the same as before or different. Without the idea of causality, we would not have the idea of an object's being identical over time. But whence the idea of causality itself? This, Hume suggests, arises precisely from the insertion of metaphors into metonymic chains.

Hume's explanation proceeds as follows. First, he traces the idea of causality to the idea of contiguity: the imagination never posits a causal connection without first noticing a contiguity in time and place between signifiers (Hume 1978, 75). Second, he notes the importance of temporal order to the idea of causality (Hume 1978, 76). Finally, he calls attention to the fact that the imagination never invokes the idea of causality without its being accompanied by a feeling of necessary connection between two signifiers (Hume 1978, 77). The mystery lies precisely here: Why this feeling of necessity?

Hume answers by appealing to the phenomenon of repetition, or what he calls "constant conjunction." Because the imagination associates resembling signifiers, and because it notices resembling patterns of contiguity (constant conjunction), it forms the habit of expecting to find one signifier followed by another. This sense of expectation is the entire secret behind the feeling of necessary connection:

> We remember to have had frequent instances of the existence of one species of objects; and also remember, that the individuals of another species of objects have always attended them, and have existed in a regular order of contiguity and succession with regard to them. Thus we remember to have seen that species of object we call *flame*, and to have felt that species of sensation we call *heat*. We likewise call to mind their constant conjunction in all past instances. Without any farther ceremony, we call the one *cause* and the other *effect*, and infer the existence of the one from that of the other. (Hume 1978, 87)

The idea of causality explains nothing. It is ultimately just a noncognitive feeling that two signifiers somehow belong together. A succinct account of this phenomenon can be found in Lacan:

> Cause is to be distinguished from that which is determinate in a chain, in other words, the *law*. . . .
>
> Whenever we speak of cause, . . . there is always something anti-conceptual, something indefinite. The phases of the moon are the cause of tides—we know this from experience, we know that the word cause is correctly used here. Or again, miasmas are the cause of fever—that doesn't mean anything either, there is a hole, and something that oscillates in the interval. In short, there is cause only in something that doesn't work. (Lacan 1978, 22)

Although Lacan invokes Kant, citing his use of the word *gap* in the *Prolegomena*, Kant himself has Hume in mind throughout his discussion of causality that appears in the *Prolegomena*. (Lacan's word is *béance*; he does not give the German, and I have been unable to locate *Lücke* in the *Prolegomena*, although it does appear in the first Critique.) For Kant, it is Hume who shows that "We cannot at all see why, in consequence of the existence of one thing, another must necessarily exist, or how the concept of such a combination can arise *a priori*" (Kant 1977, 3). Kant's aim, by contrast, is to fill this gap.

Hume calls attention to the manner in which the imagination invents an idea of causality that never fills the gap between signifiers. According to Lacan, the concept of the unconscious reveals "the gap through which neurosis recreates a harmony with a real—a real that may well not be determined" (Lacan 1978, 22). By emphasizing the role that imagination plays in constructing ideas which never harmonize with the play of signifiers, Hume opens up the question of the unconscious. Kant, however, recalls Hume's question only in order to close off the problem of the unconscious. He does so by insisting that causality is regulated by an a priori law which guarantees that there are no gaps in reality whatsoever. As Lacan points out, once the concept of causality is regulated by the concept of law, all "gaps" in the Real have been left behind: "By way of example, think of what is pictured in the law of action and reaction. There is here, one might say, a single principle. . . . There is no gap here" (Lacan 1978, 22). In point of fact, this is precisely the move that Kant (not Hume) makes—namely, the reinterpretation of causality qua gap as causality qua law. Thus, in the "Second Analogy" of the *Critique* Kant invokes "the law of the continuity of all alteration," a principle which states that "neither time nor appearance in time consists of parts which are the smallest" (A209/B254). This principle is specifically designed to preclude the possibility of there being quantum leaps of any sort in experience.

Kant further erases the gap in the Real by insisting on "the principle of universal natural science—viz., that *nothing* happens *by chance*" (Kant 1987, 256). Lacan, it is worth recalling, invokes the concept of a gap in order to rework the Aristotelian conception of *tuché*—a term usually translated in English as *chance* or in French as *hasard*, and which Lacan connects with the subject's missed encounter with the Real. *Tuché*, in other words, suggests an encounter with the gap qua gap. What remains on the order of chance is the specific accident that might instigate this encounter, and perhaps the specific manner in which a neurosis, perversion, or psychosis might result. At the level of sensibility, of course, Kant is willing to grant that there is a kind of gap in experience which is filled by the concept of causality. But whereas Hume traces the idea of causality back to the imagination, Kant insists that the idea must spring from the pure understanding. For his part, Hume simply reduces understanding and reason to habits of imagination. Ultimately, there is no law governing how we think or how we ought to think; there are only symbolic patterns which get generated and repeated.

Habits, which are formed through the binding of signifiers, both limit the free play of imagination and introduce the patterns that will govern the binding of new signifiers. The ultimate explanation of habit-formation is not the regularity of experience but the fact that the psychic apparatus constantly repeats itself in applying the principles of association to signifiers. In this relentless movement—which has no other meaning than that of a constant return to the missed Real—we can see hints of the metapsychological theory of repetition. Like Freudian repetition, Humean habit-formation takes place at a level that is more primordial than anything that appears at the level of conscious experience. In this respect, the Humean theory of habituation is completely different from the Aristotelian theory which Lacan rightly distinguishes from psychoanalytic models of character-formation (Lacan 1992, 10). Where metapsychology might be said to supplement Hume is with its theory of the trauma—of that unique encounter with the Real which, precisely because it cannot be assimilated, inaugurates a specific trajectory of character-formation.

In other respects as well, Lacan might be read as supplementing Hume's theory of the subject. Consider Lacan's description of the mirror stage and its role in constituting an ideal ego situated in the field of the Other. There is, of course, a kind of surface parallel between this account and the argument of Kant's "Refutation of Idealism," where the empirical subject's idea of itself is said to depend upon its recognition of something permanent in outer intuition. The problem with identifying the two models is that for Kant the permanent in question can only be the signified (whether substance, transcendental object, or noumenon) of a signifier. For Lacan, by contrast, the mirror image is merely a signifier with which the infant identifies. This signifier remains as a kind of permanent trace (imago), which represents the imaginary identity of the subject.

For Hume too the subject derives its idea of itself from a kind of mirror image—specifically, from the idea of the identity of objects over time. But for Hume, like Lacan, there are no such objects; there are only signifiers which are organized in such a way as to lead the imagination to presume an object to exist as the underlying signified of experience. Put otherwise, the signifier of an object is a lure which captures the gaze of that which will imagine itself to be a subject where it imagines it finds an object. For this reason, Hume traces the genesis of the idea of the self to the genesis of the signifier of an object (Hume 1978, 253).

To appreciate Hume's argument, we need to see that he is first trying to account for how a signifier comes to represent an *object* for another signifier; from there he will attempt to tackle the question concerning the idea of a subject.

Hume's explanation is fairly complicated. First, he argues that the idea of time is itself merely the idea of a succession of signifiers. Where no succession appears, there is no idea of time. Sometimes, however, a single signifier will appear simultaneously with the appearance of a succession of other signifiers. In this case, only the series of signifiers conveys the idea of time; the unchanging signifier does not. But because the unchanging signifier is contiguous with each of the signifiers that conveys the idea of time, the imagination is led to believe (i.e., feel) that the unchanging signifier was itself perceived over time. In other words, the imagination supposes there to have been a succession of identical signifiers where in fact the mind has encountered but a single signifier. In this way, the signifier in question comes to represent an object—but only, so to speak, "for" the series of successive signifiers.

Hume presumes that the idea of the subject is to be explained in the same way. But here he runs up against a difficulty, because in this case there does not seem to be any single signifier which "endures" during a succession of other signifiers.

> If any impression gives rise to the idea of self, that impression must continue invariably the same, thro' the whole course of our lives; since self is suppos'd to exist after that manner. But there is no impression constant and invariable. (Hume 1978, 251)

Hume confesses that there seems to be no other way of explaining where the idea of a subject could come from. Explaining the idea of the subject as something constituted by the function of memory seems inadequate, since memory is taken not to constitute but to discover the identity of the subject in question (Hume 1978, 262).

Of course, the conclusion that no enduring signifier can be found is supported solely by the evidence of introspection. Precisely here, we can see how Lacan supplements Hume's theory. For one way of reading Lacan's account of the mirror stage (more fruitful than treating it as an observational statement belonging to developmental psychology) would be as a kind of quasitranscendental deduction of the mirror imago, based on the supposition that only an unconscious signifier could solve Hume's enigma concerning the genesis of the idea of the subject.

Of course, even without an explicit conception of the unconscious, Hume notices the gap that separates the symbolic from the Real. By insisting on this gap, he is able to evoke the work of the unconscious via the imagination, thereby calling into question the metaphysical pretensions of the symbolic order. It is in this respect that Hume can be read retrospectively (or prospectively with Freud) as Kant's analyst; his task throughout the *Treatise* is to show the Kantian subject that its claims to invoke reason as lawgiver are all delusions.

Like the hysteric, Hume explicitly calls attention to the gap in the Real which only imagination fills. He shows not only that both the empirical ego and the symbolic order are structured like symptoms, but that the idea of law is itself but a fiction—in this way anticipating the work of Jeremy Bentham which Lacan invokes (Lacan 1992, 12). Like the schizophrenic, Hume finds himself shifting back and forth between a series of skeptical theses and a series of "normalizing" antitheses when he returns from his drawing room to human society (Hume 1978, 269). (I note, in this connection, that on my reading the Kantian theses themselves should count as skeptical, the antitheses as dogmatic.) Hume argues for the "philosophical" point that experience consists of nothing but signifiers, and yet he acknowledges that strictly speaking it is impossible to give up the "vulgar" view that experience presents us only with signifieds (objects) and nothing more (Hume 1978, 213). Unlike Kant, who resolves this schizophrenic uncertainty by passing to the stage of paranoia, Hume remains within the aporias which he brings to light.

Strictly speaking, of course, the antinomies of schizophrenia can be read as attacks against the dogmas of Cartesianism as much as the dogmas of Kantianism. Ultimately, we would have to turn from Hume's analysis of human understanding to his analysis of passions and morals in order to appreciate his resistance to the Kantian superego. Here, two arguments in particular stand out. First, anticipating Freud by almost two hundred years, Hume traces the origin of the idea of God to a process of idealization. In the end, Hume is less interested in the question of whether or not God exists than he is in the question of whether or not it is possible to form a determinate idea of the nature of God (Hume 1978, 633). In this sense, he resists the movement from the idea of the fourth antinomy to the Kantian ideal of reason.

The other argument is Hume's contention that the law itself is motivated by passion and sentiment. In other words, not only does he resist the Kantian ideal of an autonomous will that would not be determined by inclinations, he rejects the assumption that ideas of morality arise from a rejection of pathological content. In this connection, Hume heralds Freud's recognition of the libidinal roots of the superego. In making this move, Hume hearkens back to Aristotle in two respects. First, he revives the Aristotelian conception of character as the ground of action; however, he does so not by invoking a theory of substance but by giving unlimited extension to the principles of habit-formation which Aristotle invokes in the *Nicomachean Ethics*. In other words, because there is no ontological substrate—no underlying soul with innate tendencies that is acquiring its habits—Hume can develop a theory of character that is in this respect closer to Freud's than to that of Aristotle. Second, by making passion the ultimate ground of moral principles themselves, Hume maintains the possibility of treating happiness as the proper end of human activity—but in such a way as to take full account of Lacan's principal objections both to Aristotelian eudaimonism and to the specific concept of happiness advanced in ego psychology.

Lacan notes a connection between the concept of *tuché* and the concept of happiness (Lacan 1992, 13). For Aristotle in particular, happiness would result from a "good encounter" between the subject and the cosmos. For the attainment of happiness to be possible, some coordination of the desires of the subject with the order of the world would have to take place. This encounter is prepared, for Aristotle, by the right kind of habituation—the adequation of man to the world. Once we accept Freud's argument that the encounter with the Real never quite takes place, the possibility of happiness is thrown into question. It is for this reason, Lacan claims, that Freud arrives at the pessimistic conclusions of *Civilization and Its Discontents*:

> Freud doesn't for a moment consider identifying adequacy to reality with a specific good. In *Civilization and Its Discontents* he tells us that civilization or culture certainly asks too much of the subject. If there is indeed something that can be called his good or his happiness, there is nothing to be expected in that regard from the microcosm, nor moreover from the macrocosm. (Lacan 1992, 34)

Because reality is so hostile to the aims of the pleasure principle, the reality principle appears as a moral injunction impelling the subject away from the imaginary: "Reality is precarious. And it is precisely to the extent that access to it is so precarious that the commandments which trace its path are so tyrannical" (Lacan 1992, 30). Lacan in effect locates the agency of the superego at the level of the reality principle itself:

> My thesis is that the moral law, the moral command, the presence of the moral agency in our activity, insofar as it is structured by the symbolic, is that through which the real is actualized—the real as such, the weight of the real. (Lacan 1992, 20)

From here, of course, it is but a short step to Lacan's reading of Kant and Sade. Once Kant recognizes that there is nothing in the world that could be identified with a supreme good, he has no choice but to institute the categorical imperative as that which impels the subject to experience the cruelty of the Real.

The choice between Aristotle and Kant is, however, far from being exhaustive. Unlike Aristotle, Hume gives up the idea of a cosmic order to which desire might conform. Unlike Kant, on the other hand, he interprets the reality principle as a continuation of the pleasure principle rather than as an injunction against it. This, of course, makes sense. On Freud's account of the genesis of the superego, libidinal motivation (eros) is at the heart of moral experience—along with, of course, the death drive. But the death drive is invoked by Freud in order to explain a cruelty that might admit of a different explanation. In particular, it seems possible to trace the origin of the cruelty of the superego to the paranoiac foreclosure of the feminine *cogito,* a foreclosure that makes enjoyment possible only through the suffering of sublimity. Were it possible to deconstruct the antinomies of schizophrenia, might it not be possible that this type of cruelty could be alleviated? For the Humean schizo, *jouissance* might be "beyond the pleasure principle" precisely as the experience of the beautiful.

Ever since Kant—the legacy we receive in belonging to the era of the superego—eudaimonism has been under attack. In strict Kantian fashion, we are said to have only two alternatives: either we pursue an animalistic and selfish hedonism or we put the demands of duty above all else. Leaving aside the questionable presumption that there is anything about being human that would make us different from animals—a point which Hume explicitly calls into question (contra Lacan) by showing that all animals are constituted in the order of the signifier (Hume 1978, 176ff)—the terms of this alleged opposition are themselves quite dubious. As usually represented, the choice of happiness over duty is said to have no way of avoiding the evils of sadism. Against this view, Lacan makes the following humorous remark:

> Before coming here today I read in Jones a kind of celebration of the sublime virtues of social pressure, without which our contemporaries, our fellow humans, would be vain, egotistical, sordid, sterile, etc. One is tempted to comment in the margin, "What are they but that?" (Lacan 1992, 25)

More important, as Lacan shows in "Kant with Sade," it is precisely the choice of Kantian duty that coincides most closely with the principles of Sadean perversity. Lacan's point is not that the Kantian subject can no more avoid acting from inclinations than can the Sadean subject. On the contrary, his point is that it is precisely insofar as the Kantian subject succeeds in rising above its inclinations that it resembles the cruel Sadean. Moreover, as Freud himself points out, the primary function of the superego is not to ensure that moral actions are performed; this is merely its pretext. The primary function of the superego is to exercise cruelty. This is why the stronger a person's superego is, the guiltier he or she will feel (*SE* XIX, 54).

What exactly is the moral of Lacan's essay then? Is it, as most commentators seem to have suggested, that there is no escaping the logic of the superego? Taking up the question of whether a Spinozist ethics of love might be tenable, Lacan says:

> This position is not tenable *for us.* Experience shows us that Kant is more true, and I have proved that his theory of consciousness, when he writes of practical reason, is sustained only by giving a specification of the moral law which, looked at more closely, is simply desire in its pure state, that very desire that culminates in the sacrifice, strictly speaking, of everything that is the object of love in one's human tenderness—I would say, not only in the rejection of the pathological object, but also in its sacrifice and murder. (Lacan 1978, 275–76; my italics)

*For us*: certainly Lacan diagnoses our age as a Kantian one. Nonetheless the question remains: Are we to treat the superego as a transcendental law in response to which the best we can do is to learn to enjoy the desire that it instills in us? Or could it be that we are living in psychotic times?

Žižek has argued that the "rational," manifest, daytime law of the symbolic order is necessarily supported by an "irrational," hidden, nightly law of the superego (Žižek 1994, 54). This suggests that there can be no ethics without the cruelty of the superego. In making such a supposition, might we not once again flip from the position of the hysterical analyst of Kant back into an ever more stringent Kantianism? I take it that Žižek gives us a brilliant and accurate analysis of the structure of lived experience in the era of the superego, but I question whether we should presume that this structure is transcendental. (In the end, I am not sure where Žižek himself comes down on this question.)

Suppose, extending my earlier suggestion about the trajectory of modern philosophical thought, we were to read the series of symptoms presented in Kant's *Critique* as a phylogenetic sequence rather than as a synchronic account of transcendental structures of experience. (In fact, this is precisely what strikes Hegel when he reads Kant—that Kant has laid out a structure which is in fact a genesis; this discovery prompts Hegel to write the *Phenomenology of Spirit.*) On such a reading of Kant, the dawn of humanity would begin with the hysterical identification with the bodily imago of outer intuition. From there would develop the obsessional shift from space to time, and the perverse subsumption of the hysterical under obsessional laws. The obsessional's "I think," withdrawing its cathexes from spatial objects, would become narcissistic. The return of the repressed at the level of the antinomies would mark the onset of schizophrenia. Here I would stress the connection I have tried to draw between hysteria and schizophrenia; in effect, the schizophrenic would be the subject whose obsessional laws have been suspended, thereby allowing for a dialectical "conflict" between hysterical (feminine) and obsessional (masculine) symptoms. The possibility for a reconfiguration of the relationship between the hysterical and the obsessional would arise here. The failure to achieve a reconciliation would lead first to Humean melancholia and then to the paranoiac *Verwerfung* which Kant inaugurates.

This phylogenetic narrative has some striking parallels with the narrative that Freud suggests in his recently discovered metapsychological paper. Freud imagines the following series: "anxiety hysteria—conversion hysteria—obsessional neurosis—dementia praecox [schizophrenia]—paranoia—melancholia-mania" (Freud 1987, 12). The only significant difference between the Kantian and Freudian sequences would be that Freud places the melancholia-mania dyad after paranoia. However, he immediately adds, "melancholia-mania permits no certain ranking with respect to time" (Freud 1987, 12). Freud's uncertainty here serves my purposes well, for it suggests the possibility that Humean melancholia can be thought of as both that which precipitates the shift to Kantian paranoia, and as that which arises in the wake of Kantianism.

Freud's reminder that melancholia and mania go hand in hand also serves to temper the sort of enthusiasm—precisely what Kant calls *Schwärmerei*—that could also result from the schizophrenic impulse. Obviously, the history of ill-fated attempts to displace capitalist paranoia would have to be interrogated in this light. The problem is that Kant leaves us with the choice of either paranoia or mania—which might well be the case in the age of the superego, but which might be precisely why we need to return to the position of the schizophrenic in order to imagine whether alternative relations between space and time might be thinkable. Perhaps humanity can create new, nonobsessional, perversions?

If Hume leaves us with any fundamental principle of ethics, it might also be framed, with Žižek, in terms of a perverse "Enjoy your symptom!" But it would not be a command of morality in the Kantian sense; it would be a principle of passion based on the possibility of a "pleasure in ethics"—a postanalytic eudaimonistic "Enjoy!" rather than a Kantian/Schreberian "You must . . . !" Perhaps, in light of the work of Irigaray, it is possible to rework Herbert Marcuse's call for a reconciliation of the demands of eros and civilization. And perhaps this is our only nonmanic alternative to the present reign of paranoiac cruelty. For the Kantian superego, as Lacan points out, can only insist—and will increasingly insist—on the complete annihilation of everything that falls under the name of passion, chance, and love.

# Works Cited

Note: All references to the *Standard Edition of the Complete Psychological Works of Sigmund Freud* are cited in the body of the text as *SE* followed by the volume and page numbers. In accordance with standard practice, all references to the *Critique of Pure Reason* are cited in the body of the text with reference to the "A" and "B" editions.


Abraham, Nicolas, and Maria Torok. *The Shell and the Kernel.* Vol. 1. Edited and translated by Nicholas Rand. Chicago: The University of Chicago Press, 1994.

Andreas-Salomé, Lou. *The Freud Journal of Lou Andreas-Salomé.* Translated by Stanley A. Leavey. New York: Basic Books, 1964.

———, and Sigmund Freud. *Sigmund Freud and Lou Andreas-Salomé: Letters.* Edited by Ernst Pfeiffer. Translated by William and Elaine Robson-Scott. New York: W. W. Norton and Co., 1985.

Aquila, Richard. "Self-Consciousness, Self-Determination, and Imagination in Kant." *Topoi* 7 (1988) 65–79.

Barr, Stephen. *Experiments in Topology.* New York: Dover, 1989.

Brennan, Teresa. *History after Lacan.* New York: Routledge, 1993.

Butler, Judith. *Gender Trouble: Feminism and the Subversion of Identity.* New York: Routledge, 1990.

Cassam, Quassim. "Inner Sense, Body Sense, and Kant's 'Refutation of Idealism.' " *European Journal of Philosophy* 1, no. 2 (1993), 111–27.

Cavell, Stanley. "Freud and Philosophy: A Fragment." *Critical Inquiry* 13, no. 2 (1987), 386–93.

Copjec, Joan. *Read My Desire: Lacan against the Historicists.* Cambridge: MIT Press, 1995.

Cutrofello, Andrew. *Discipline and Critique: Kant, Poststructuralism, and the Problem of Resistance.* Albany: State University of New York Press, 1994.

———. "Quine and the Inscrutability of Languages." *International Studies in Philosophy* 24, no. 1 (1992), 33–46.

Deleuze, Gilles. *Kant's Critical Philosophy.* Translated by Hugh Tomlinson and Barbara Habberjam. Minneapolis: University of Minnesota Press, 1983.

———. *Nietzsche and Philosophy.* Translated by Hugh Tomlinson. New York: Columbia University Press, 1983.

———, and Félix Guattari. *Anti-Oedipus: Capitalism and Schizophrenia.* Translated by Robert Hurley, Mark Seem, and Helen R. Lane. Minneapolis: University of Minnesota Press, 1983.

———. *A Thousand Plateaus: Capitalism and Schizophrenia.* Translated by Brian Massumi. Minneapolis: University of Minnesota Press, 1987.

———. *What is Philosophy?* Translated by Hugh Tomlinson and Graham Burchell. New York: Columbia University Press, 1994.

Descartes, René. *Meditations on First Philosophy.* 3d ed. Translated by Donald A. Cress. Indianapolis: Hackett, 1993.

Deutsch, Helene. *Neuroses and Character Types: Clinical Psychoanalytic Studies.* New York: International Universities Press, 1965.

Dummett, Michael. *Truth and Other Enigmas.* Cambridge: Harvard University Press, 1978.

Enriquez, Micheline. "Paranoiac Fantasies: Sexual Difference, Homosexuality, Law of the Father." In *Psychosis and Sexual Identity: Toward a Post-Analytic View of the Schreber Case.* Edited by David B. Allison, et al. Albany: State University of New York Press, 1988. 102–29.

Freud, Sigmund. *A Phylogenetic Fantasy: Overview of the Transference Neuroses.* Edited by Ilse Grubrich-Simitis. Translated by Axel Hoffer and Peter T. Hoffer. Cambridge: Harvard University Press, 1987.

———. *The Standard Edition of the Complete Psychological Works of Sigmund Freud.* 24 vols. Edited and translated by James Strachey, in collaboration with Anna Freud, assisted by Alix Strachey and Alan Tyson. London: Hogarth Press and the Institute of Psychoanalysis, 1953–74.

Gibbons, Sarah L. *Kant's Theory of Imagination: Bridging Gaps in Judgement and Experience.* New York: Oxford University Press, 1994.

Habermas, Jürgen. *Knowledge and Human Interests.* Translated by Jeremy J. Shapiro. Boston: Beacon, 1972.

Hegel, G. W. F. *Phenomenology of Spirit.* Translated by A. V. Miller. New York: Oxford University Press, 1977.

Heidegger, Martin. *Kant and the Problem of Metaphysics.* Translated by Richard Taft. Indianapolis: Indiana University Press, 1990.

Hengehold, Laura. "The Body's Contribution to Inner Sense in Kant's Refutation of Idealism." Presented at *Openings: The Space of Thinking,* Vanderbilt University, 26–27 January 1996.

Hume, David. *A Treatise of Human Nature.* 2d ed. Edited by P. H. Nidditch. New York: Oxford University Press, 1978.

Irigaray, Luce. *An Ethics of Sexual Difference.* Translated by Carolyn Burke and Gillian C. Gill. Ithaca: Cornell University Press, 1993.

———. *Speculum of the Other Woman.* Translated by Gillian C. Gill. Ithaca: Cornell University Press, 1985.

Kant, Immanuel. *Anthropology from a Pragmatic Point of View.* Translated by Mary J. Gregor. The Hague: Martinus Nijhoff, 1974.

———. *Critique of Judgment.* Translated by Werner S. Pluhar. Indianapolis: Hackett, 1987.

———. *Critique of Pure Reason.* Translated by Norman Kemp Smith. New York: St. Martin's Press, 1965.

———. *Grounding for the Metaphysics of Morals.* Translated by James W. Ellington. Indianapolis: Hackett, 1981.

———. *Kritik der reinen Vernunft.* 2 vols. Frankfurt am Main: Suhrkamp, 1956.
———. *Metaphysical Foundations of Natural Science.* In Kant, *Philosophy of Material Nature.* Translated by James W. Ellington. Indianapolis: Hackett, 1985.
———. *Observations on the Feeling of the Beautiful and Sublime.* Translated by John T. Goldthwait. Berkeley: University of California Press, 1991.
———. *Prolegomena to any Future Metaphysics.* Translated by James W. Ellington. Indianapolis: Hackett, 1977.
———. *Religion within the Limits of Reason Alone.* Translated by Theodore M. Greene and Hoyt H. Hudson. New York: Harper and Row, 1960.
———. *Theoretical Philosophy, 1755–1770.* Translated and edited by David Walford. New York: Cambridge University Press, 1992.
Kitcher, Patricia. *Kant's Transcendental Psychology.* New York: Oxford University Press, 1990.
Kripke, Saul A. *Naming and Necessity.* Cambridge: Harvard University Press, 1980.
Lacan, Jacques. *Écrits.* Paris: Éditions du Seuil, 1966.
———. *Écrits: A Selection.* Translated by Alan Sheridan. New York: W. W. Norton and Co., 1977.
———. *The Four Fundamental Concepts of Psycho-Analysis.* Edited by Jacques-Alain Miller. Translated by Alan Sheridan. New York: W. W. Norton and Co., 1978.
———. "Kant with Sade." Translated by James Swenson, Jr. *October* 51 (Winter 1989), 55–75.
———. *The Seminar of Jacques Lacan.* Book I: *Freud's Papers on Technique, 1953–1954.* Edited by Jacques-Alain Miller. Translated by John Forrester. New York: W. W. Norton and Co., 1991b.
———. *The Seminar of Jacques Lacan.* Book III: *The Psychoses, 1955–1956.* Edited by Jacques-Alain Miller. Translated by Russell Grigg. New York: W. W. Norton and Co., 1993.
———. *The Seminar of Jacques Lacan.* Book VII: *The Ethics of Psychoanalysis.* Edited by Jacques-Alain Miller. Translated by Dennis Porter. New York: W. W. Norton and Co., 1992.
———. *Le séminaire de Jacques Lacan.* Livre XVII: *L'envers de la psychanalyse.* Edited by Jacques-Alain Miller. Paris: Éditions du Seuil, 1991a.
———. *Le séminaire de Jacques Lacan.* Livre XI: *Les quatre concepts fondamentaux de la psychanalyse.* Edited by Jacques-Alain Miller. Paris: Éditions du Seuil, 1973.
———, et al. *Feminine Sexuality.* Edited by Juliet Mitchell and Jacqueline Rose. New York: W. W. Norton and Co., 1985.
Lingis, Alphonso. "The Din of the Celestial Birds or Why I Crave to Become a Woman." In *Psychosis and Sexual Identity: Toward a Post-Analytic View of the Schreber Case.* Edited by David B. Allison, et al. Albany: State University of New York Press, 1988. 130–42.
Marcuse, Herbert. *Eros and Civilization: A Philosophical Inquiry into Freud.* Boston: Beacon, 1974.
Nerlich, Graham. "Hands, Knees, and Absolute Space." *Journal of Philosophy* 70, no. 12 (June 1973), 337–51.
Nietzsche, Friedrich. *Beyond Good and Evil.* Translated by Walter Kaufmann. New York: Vintage, 1966.

———. *The Gay Science.* Translated by Walter Kaufmann. New York: Vintage, 1974.
Palmquist, Stephen. "A Priori Knowledge in Perspective: Naming, Necessity and the Analytic A Posteriori." *Review of Metaphysics* 41 (December 1987), 255–82.
Quine, W. V. *Ontological Relativity and Other Essays.* New York: Columbia University Press, 1969.
———. "Two Dogmas of Empiricism." In *From a Logical Point of View.* 2d ed. Cambridge: Harvard University Press, 1980.
Reich, Klaus. *The Completeness of Kant's Table of Judgments.* Translated by Jane Kneller and Michael Losonsky. Stanford: Stanford University Press, 1992.
Ricoeur, Paul. *Freud and Philosophy: An Essay on Interpretation.* Translated by Denis Savage. New Haven: Yale University Press, 1970.
Sartre, Jean-Paul. *Existentialism and Human Emotions.* Translated by Bernard Frechtman and Hazel E. Barnes. New York: Wisdom Library, 1957.
Whitebook, Joel. "Hypostatizing Thanatos: Lacan's Analysis of the Ego." *Constellations* 1, no. 2 (October 1994), 214–30.
Willett, Cynthia. *Maternal Ethics and Other Slave Narratives.* New York: Routledge, 1995.
Žižek, Slavoj. *Enjoy Your Symptom!: Jacques Lacan in Hollywood and Out.* New York: Routledge, 1992.
———. *The Metastases of Enjoyment: Six Essays on Woman and Causality.* New York: Verso, 1994.
———. *Tarrying with the Negative: Kant, Hegel, and the Critique of Ideology.* Durham: Duke University Press, 1993.
———. "'Woman is one of the names-of-the-father' . . ." *Lacanian Ink* 10 (Fall 1995), 24–39.

# Index